REEDS
MARITIME FLAG
HANDBOOK

3RD EDITION

Edited by
MIRANDA DELMAR-MORGAN

T0017138

REEDS

LONDON · OXFORD · NEW YORK · NEW DELHI · SYDNEY

REEDS
Bloomsbury Publishing Plc
50 Bedford Square, London, WC1B 3DP, UK
29 Earlsfort Terrace, Dublin 2, Ireland

BLOOMSBURY, REEDS, and the Reeds logo are trademarks of Bloomsbury
Publishing Plc

First published in Great Britain 2006
Second edition 2015
This edition published 2022

Based on Reeds Maritime Flags © Sir Peter Johnson 2002

Copyright © Miranda Delmar-Morgan, 2006, 2015, 2022

Miranda Delmar-Morgan has asserted her right under the Copyright, Designs
and Patents Act, 1988, to be identified as Author of this work

For legal purposes the Acknowledgements on p. vi
constitute an extension of this copyright page

A catalogue record for this book is available from the British Library

Library of Congress Cataloguing-in-Publication data has been applied for.

ISBN: PB: 978-1-4729-9445-5; ePub: 978-1-4729-9446-2; ePDF: 978-1-4729-9447-9

2 4 6 8 10 9 7 5 3 1

Typeset in 8pt on 11pt Myriad Light by carrdesignstudio.com
Printed and bound in India by Replika Press Pvt. Ltd.

To find out more about our authors and books visit www.bloomsbury.com
and sign up for our newsletters

CONTENTS

Vessels of all shapes and sizes, sail and power, pleasure boats, working ships and naval vessels all display flags for one reason or another. They are either indicating their nationalities, their intentions (such as leaving port), their current operations (such as having divers in the water), their racing class, etc.

Most of the content of this book applies to flags wherever they are used afloat, and also when used ashore in a maritime capacity. This little book is focused on the needs of yachts and smaller working craft, and it is intended to be a handy ready reference for their crews to consult quickly and easily. Navies and shipping lines have their own codes of use and are unlikely to need any advice contained in this book. Every so often you will encounter their practises, though, so it is as well to be able to recognise and interpret their signals where necessary. Much signalling has been obviated by the use of VHF but even in our modern age visual signals remain an important tool for communications on the water.

There are technical implications to certain words in the English language used when flags, or *colours*, are shown. These words include *fly* and *wear*. Strictly speaking, a ship or boat wears a flag and the mariner flies a flag. Other terms such as *display*, *hoist*, *show*, and *rig* are also used but for easy reading they should be considered more or less interchangeable. The word 'yacht' here, unless specified, can be taken to mean either a sailing or motor yacht.

Please note that all the flags throughout the book are for illustrative purposes. Their proportions may not be exactly to scale.

Some countries occasionally discuss designing an entirely new flag, and those with British affiliations vote from time to time on whether or not to drop the British Union flag from the

Acknowledgements

canton. We have endeavoured to ascertain that the flags in this edition are correct at the time of going to press.

Whilst it might look odd to see flags of landlocked countries included in these pages it is possible that they are members of the International Maritime Organization and do have ships at sea. Therefore you may encounter their flags afloat.

Acknowledgements

Grateful thanks are extended to Cdr Henry Buchanan, Cdr Justin Wood, Capt William Whatley, Boyd Holmes, Steve McInnis, Jonno Barrett, John Bartlett and Hunter Peace who all made useful comments and suggestions.

Illustrations

French naval ensign 1790–4: Rama, Creative Commons

Symbols and banners pre-date our modern flags. The Chinese Emperor, Chou had a white cloth carried before him in 1122BC. In approximately 100BC the Romans had vexillum, which was a horizontal banner suspended from a cross piece on a vertical spear that could quickly be engaged as a weapon if necessary. From the Latin 'vexillum' we have inherited the term 'vexillology' in English to describe the study of flags. The Bayeux Tapestry in Bayeux, Normandy shows opposing forces at the Battle of Hastings in 1066 carrying *gonfalons*, war flags on vertical poles. Then, and later, banners of war could be seen flying from ships and they eventually evolved into what we understand as flags. They were more about identifying warlords than declaring a nationality, and those representing a monarch, ruler, pope, duke or an emperor became known as *standards*. Royal standards exist today, usually flown from palaces and baronial stately homes.

A perusal of historical flags shows that they chart the history of a nation, the union of different identities, such as the Scottish and the English (see page 39 regarding the Union flag), or the abandonment of a monarchical system, such as a revolution and deposition of a monarch. When colonies have gained independence from their colonial powers they have usually created a new flag, often dropping the colours of their colonisers in order to indicate their freedom. So flags often reflect a country's history and political changes.

Britain

The Union flag is explained on page 39, but see also below. Like France there were white flags with royal arms to mark royal ships, and ensigns to indicate squadrons of the fleet. Some had stripes, sometimes the red cross of St George was used, and monarchs had their own standards raised when they were nearby. In mediaeval times the three long lions of England arrived from Normandy with William the Conqueror in 1066. At one point in the fifteenth century the fleur-de-lis of France was quartered with the lions because the kings of England claimed

A short history

the throne of France. Queen Elizabeth I had a lion treading on the French lily and the Latin tag meaning 'always the same', which the Tudor monarchs followed.

This all changed when James VI of Scotland also became James I of England and the thrones were united. The red Scottish lion rampant was quartered with the English triple lions. Later the Irish harp was added, and this made up today's royal standard. Wales, conquered by England in the thirteenth century, has never appeared on the royal standard because it is a principality. It appears on the arms of the Prince of Wales, not on those of the king or queen. James I wanted a new flag for his new union. The English red cross of St George and the Scottish white cross of St Andrews were united after much discussion about which should go on top of the other. In 1801 with the Act of Union with Ireland the St Patrick's cross of red diagonals was added, giving the British the Union flag of today. Since a royal order of 1634 only His or Her Majesty's ships may fly the union flag, and this remains the case.

In Stuart times the navy began flying blue, red and white ensigns usually with either the Union flag or else just the English or Scottish flag in the canton. By the end of the seventeenth century British merchant vessels were flying the red ensign and this became officially accepted from 1674.

Ships of the British East India Company, a major trading company, flew various striped flags. The Honourable East India Company ensigns had first the St George's cross until 1707, and then the current Union flag in the canton with thirteen stripes.

East India Company ensign 1707–1800

The number of stripes had varied but was usually an uneven number in order for there to be red at the top and bottom. It was the thirteen stripe version which got incorporated into the early American ensign.

At the Battle of Trafalgar in 1805 Nelson ordered the whole of the British fleet to fly white ensigns in order to distinguish them from the enemy, however the use of all three, red, white and blue ensigns, continued until 1864 when it was finally declared that the only naval ensign should be the white one. All other British and colonial vessels were instructed to fly red ensigns but various government departments were allocated blue ensigns or defaced red or blue ones. A merchant Shipping Act of 1894 rationalised them and also laid out guidance regarding defaced ensigns.

The white ensign was sanctioned for use by some yacht clubs in the early nineteenth century; in 1842 however the white ensign was withdrawn from all but the Royal Yacht Squadron, with the exception of the Royal Western Yacht Club of Ireland, which got overlooked, but finally had it withdrawn in 1858. As a concession to appease some of these yacht clubs, and with increasing royal patronage, some were permitted to apply for defaced red or blue ensigns. The Ministry of Defence has for several decades stated that there will be no further special ensigns.

America

Many North American colonists were Puritans from England, which meant that any flags followed English customs until the Boston Tea Party of 1773. When the American Revolution became an armed insurrection in 1775 various symbols

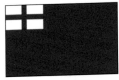

Red ensign 1620–1707

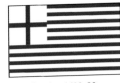

Striped ensign 1600–30

A short history

appeared, the most famous one being the rattlesnake with the words 'Dont Tread On Me' (sic) (see page 39). Another was a red ensign with the words 'Liberty and Union'.

The old red ensign with motto

New England flag 1686

At the end of 1775 a meeting took place and it was pointed out that the thirteen stripes on the East India Company flag could conveniently represent the thirteen colonies. This resulted in what was called the Cambridge Flag, since it was hoisted in Cambridge, Massachusetts in January 1776 with George Washington present. It is also known as the Union Flag. After the Declaration of Independence the British Union flag in the

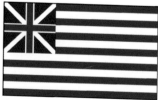

Great Union or Cambridge flag

Stars and Stripes after 1795

canton had to go. It was replaced with thirteen stars for each of the declared independent states at the time. In April 1818 the Congress passed 'An Act to establish the flag of the United States'. It simply stated that the flag and ensign were to be the thirteen red and white stripes and a star would be added to the blue canton every time a new state was added to the union. There were twenty five changes between 1818 and 1960, Hawaii being the last to be added. It has settled at 50 stars with the thirteen stripes of the original states.

Germany

Since Germany was not a unified nation but a collection of kingdoms, dukedoms and provinces up to the time of Napoleon, flags can be presumed to have been the local ruler's banner. The Hanseatic League towns of the north, such as Hamburg, Bremen, Lubeck and probably Stralsund, among others, had a red and white ensign with stripes. Hanover closely aligned with Britain since the Elector of Hanover became King George I, and had the British red ensign with a defaced canton (white or gold galloping horse on a red rectangle).

After the wars against Napoleon it was the Kingdom of Prussia that emerged as the dominant German state and the 'Holy Roman Empire' faded. Prussia followed the royal tradition of European kings using a white flag. To this was added the crowned black Prussian eagle and the black iron cross was placed in the canton. There were war and merchant ensigns with variations on this theme.

A short history

After the defeat of France in 1871 the King of Prussia was crowned Emperor of Germany (Kaiser) at Versailles and new flags were needed for a new empire. History and geography merged to create a merchant ensign with black, white and red stripes. Black for Prussia, white for the emperor or king, and red for the old Hansa. The naval ensign emulated the British habit of using white ensigns for royal and naval ships. After 1918, and with the Kaiser gone, the new Weimar Republic created a German state flag of black, red and gold. The white for royalty was dropped. The merchant flag was a compromise and kept the black, white and red, but also had the Weimar flag in the canton.

Naval ensign 1903–21

Naval ensign 1935–45

When the Nazi Party came to power in 1933 it abolished the Weimar symbols of its political enemy. The merchant ensign returned to the imperial version of three stripes. Two years later, in 1935, both the national flag and the merchant ensign were changed to the 'Hakenkreuz', meaning a hooked cross, with a large black swastika on a white circle. After 1945 the swastika was declared an illegal emblem and remains illegal. West Germany returned to Weimar colours, East Germany overlaid them with some communist symbols. After unification the

Admiral flag

Vice Admiral flag

Rear Admiral flag

national flag and merchant ensign settled as horizontal black, red and gold stripes and this has held for longer than any other German flag since 1871.

Naval ensign 1948 to the present day   Merchant ensign

The German naval ensign emulates the Scandinavian use of swallowtails, and the Prussian eagle on a gold shield has survived in the centre. The Iron Cross is used by admirals and remains a symbol of the Luftwaffe.

France

The fleur-de-lis was the symbol of France and French kings. French royal ships had at least three fleur-de-lis on their flags. They also had a white cross on a blue background. Some commercial ships simply carried their regional flags. The French Revolution of 1789 cleared away the flags from the old kingdom. The red and blue colours of Paris were added to the traditional French white in the shape of the tricolour in vertical stripes and the Constituent Assembly of France ordered this flag and

The Lilies (Standard of Charles V)

7

A short history

Naval ensign 1790–4

ensign in October 1790. Originally the red stripe was nearest to the mast, or hoist. In 1794 the colours were rearranged to the present arrangement with the red furthest away, and the red was subsequently made a slightly wider band to counter the diminishing effect of perspective.

French warships continued using the white flag with its royal connotations for some time until the new admirals of the revolution started putting the tricolour in the canton with a plain white field. At first the tricolour was a jack but from 1794 it became the ensign. The white flag of royalty was restored after the fall of Napoleon Bonaparte and lasted until the fall of the French monarchy in 1830. Since then the tricolour has been both the ensign and the country flag. Flags with stripes are said to represent a nation that has gone through a revolution but there are numerous exceptions to this rule.

Flags have been in use for a long time. The Romans hung textiles from crossbars and raised spears decorated with patterns and we have all been doing much the same ever since.

When Neil Armstrong landed on the moon, the first thing he did was to erect the Stars and Stripes. It appears that the top edge of the flag (head) was stiffened with a cane to prevent it from drooping on a windless planet. The fact that it should stand out proudly and be easy to 'read' was obviously considered important. The flag crossed all language barriers.

So flags provide a picture – but not always a welcome one. Every so often a flag representing an invading nation is burned in the streets of an occupied territory. The images are flashed around the world and it is clear that the locals don't like the visitors. Flags can be loaded with significance and arouse strong passions.

In the UK in 1997, following the death of Diana, Princess of Wales, an outcry arose in the popular press that the royal standard above the monarch's residence should be flown at half mast. Other flags around the country had been half-masted. The authorities pointed out that the royal standard signifies the presence of the sovereign and is always flown fully hoisted. Even when a king or queen dies, the royal standard is not half-masted because, on the death of the monarch, he or she is instantly succeeded by his or her heir. The standard therefore immediately represents the new head of state.

Such explanations fell on deaf ears with the tabloid press, which was determined to pursue this story. Quite a clever compromise was reached whereby a different flag (actually the Union flag) was hoisted on the mast which, until then, had displayed the royal standard. This second flag was then lowered to half mast instead and the royal standard, wilfully misunderstood by the people, was removed from the fray. This was quite a serious problem for the British Monarchy. So whilst the tradition of flying flags is ancient the dilemmas they raise will always remain modern.

What is a flag?

Their usage and meaning varies, depending on whether they are ashore or afloat. When flags are shown at harbour offices, seamen's training schools, lifeboat houses and yacht clubs, the practice followed is, as far as practicable, the same as on board ship. Mostly flag etiquette has been laid down by one navy or another and small craft skippers, such as ourselves, have inherited it. Sometimes we use it and sometimes we don't. Some of it is a matter of etiquette, some of it is antiquated, but quite a lot of it is still in current use. More important though is the fact that some flag lore has become enshrined in international law and if nothing else you do at least need to know your legal obligations.

Customs and traditions of the sea

Most flag use at sea is derived from custom and tradition. Sometimes it is voluntary, often it is vague. It varies from one country to another, and some countries get much more upset about their flags than others.

Professional ships have their own traditional usage. Yachts should consult almanacs or follow club rules. There are various flag websites listed in the Appendix. The Royal Yachting Association and Cruising Association are a mine of information for those going abroad. Generally, it is wise to avoid extraneous flags, pennants and ensigns. They are likely to be wrong, and others may strain to identify a signal that is meaningless. Other customs and traditions cover not only the flag itself, but also when, how, and where it is hoisted.

So this book is for those of you who don't really care very much what you fly, but sometimes need to know, and for those who do care what you fly and want to get it right.

Most flags for use at sea are widely available from manufacturers, ship and yacht chandlers and websites. Special ensigns, however, are usually ordered through their particular yacht club.

Seagoing flags are nowadays made of woven or knitted polyester, which dries quickly and is hard-wearing. The design is either dyed into the fabric then stitched to hold each separate colour component, or simply printed on. Printed flags look and are cheap. Obviously if you leave a flag flying day and night you will shorten its life. Dirty, tatty flags look terrible and should be replaced.

Shapes

Three shapes are common in sea flags: *rectangular* (which includes *square*, but that is unusual), *swallowtail* and *pennant* (Fig 1).

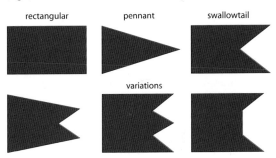

Fig 1 Shapes.

The pennant (or pendant) is triangular, but there are naval and other pennants which are much longer and closer in shape to streamers. The swallowtail is a rectangle with the end notched out. There are variations of this such as a 'sloping' top and bottom so that it is more like a pennant with the end cut. More subtle is a flat inner corner accommodating a stripe (Danish naval ensign). There can also be rare multiple tails, again found in Scandinavia.

Parts of a flag

A flag has technical names for its various areas and edges. On a rectangular flag the dimension of the long side is called the *length*; the dimension of the short side (against the flag pole) is the *breadth* or the *hoist*. The top edge can also be called the *head*. The bottom edge can be called the bottom or the *foot* (as on a sail). The part flapping in the breeze is the *fly*. A section

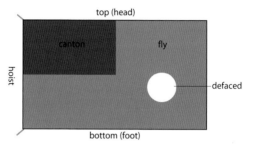

Fig 2 Nomenclature.

of the flag to which reference will frequently be made in this book is the *canton*. This is the upper corner nearest the point of suspension. Usually it consists of a quarter of the flag. *Field* or *ground* describes the background colour of the flag.

Defaced flags

Whilst the term 'defaced' usually has negative connotations implying damage, in the context of flags it actually means 'embellished'. This usually means that there has been an addition to the normal country flag. For instance the three stripes of the Spanish flag may be seen with a crown or the royal coat of arms.

The proportions of a rectangular flag vary, and specific ensigns and national flags have their own exact requirements. British flags have a proportion of 1:2 and this applies to all British-based official flags and ensigns. The Stars and Stripes has a ratio of 50:95. The French *tricolore* and others are in the very different proportion of 2:3.

Sizes

By tradition, British flag makers' measurements are in yards and multiples of yards, defying most length conventions. European makers will obviously use metric spacing. One leading firm produces its ensigns as half-yard, three-quarters yard, one yard, one-and-a-half, two, etc. Burgees are likely to be supplied in inches, the following rounded numbers being practical: 9 inches, 12, 15, 18, 24, 30, 36, etc (0.23m, 0.30m, 0.38m, 0.45m, 0.60m, 0.76m, 0.91m).

The International Code of Signals flags (see page 62) are in the proportion of 2:3, so a typical size would be 12 x 18 inches (0.30 x 0.45m). Numeral pennants will be twice as long. If code flags are to be read properly then the size of the flag is what matters and not the size of the vessel. However, if they are only used in harbour or for dressing ship and not for 'serious' signalling, then they can be quite small and therefore cheaper. One or two sizable signal flags which describe emergency or urgent situations might be a good compromise. The size given for visibility is 48 inches (1.25m). This is quite big: try code flag standard sizes of 30 inches (0.76m) or 36 inches (0.91m). A usual size for a small yacht is 12 inches (0.30m) by 18 inches (0.45m). When equipping any vessel with flags, the question of the sizes is invariably a problem, and flags look much bigger in your hands than they do aloft.

Sizes

US and UK yacht clubs conventionally give as a guide for ensigns (in defiance of metrication) one inch (2.54cm) on the fly of the ensign to 12 inches (30cm) of length overall of the vessel. Cdr L Hamilton-Stokes, RN, wrote that the fly should be one half of an inch (1.27cm) for each foot (30cm) of the length of the highest truck above the waterline. An average 10.5m yacht with a 15m mast would therefore fly a 24 inch (61cm) burgee. The New York Yacht Club also recommends these proportions for sailing yachts to its members, and half an inch for each foot of overall length on power boats. European boats appear to go in for a smaller scale.

American sailors are particularly respectful of the Stars and Stripes and tend to have oversized ensigns, though the flag should not trail in the water. Modern sailing yachts have short overhangs, so the ensign can be larger in proportion to the actual length. This applies to ensign staffs aft. Where the ensign is on a short yard on a power vessel, on the gaff of a mainsail (rare) or on a backstay, then the ensign should be smaller.

House flags, private signals and courtesy ensigns

These flags are smaller. The miniature courtesy flags sometimes seen hoisted, are not very polite to the visited nation and may cause problems in some countries. The house flag or private signal is a rectangular version of the burgee, in respect of size, and can be accorded similar dimensions.

Size of flags

LOA (ft)	Ensign	Burgee	House	Courtesy	Jacks
21–26	¾ yd	15″	6″ x 9″	7″	14″ x 21″
27–34	1 yd	15″	8″ x 12″	8″	18″ x 27″
35–42	1¼ yd	18″	10″ x 15″	10″	20″ x 30″
43–50	1½ yd	24″	12″ x 18″	12″	27″ x 40″
51–60	1¾ yd	30″	15″ x 22″	15″	32″ x 48″

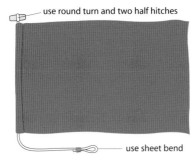

use round turn and two half hitches

use sheet bend

Fig 3 Securing.

Securing flags

Flags come with some system for hoisting, usually a line is sewn into the hoist edge. The top corner of this may have a wooden toggle, or the line is lashed or sewn into a loop. At the bottom corner will be the line, say one foot (30cm) or so, cut off and whipped (Fig 3).

To use this for an ensign on a staff, take the halyard with a round turn and two half hitches around the toggle or the loop. A bowline is not suitable as there will be too much length. The line at the bottom is secured to the other end of the halyard with a sheet bend. It can then be hoisted.

An alternative is the Inglefield clip (Fig 4). This is a simple, secure link and has long been used by professionals to link flags where they are below each other as a signal. The clip would also be on the ends of the halyard. They are very quick to attach and release, very secure when aloft, but less suitable for small boats with only occasional signalling. The yacht burgee is treated quite differently.

Fig 4 The Inglefield clip.

Securing flags

All flags when not in use should have dry secure stowage. Larger vessels have dedicated pigeonholes. A yachtsman's alternative is the flag wallet (Fig 5). This is usually used to store the International Code of Signals, but it can be used for other flags. It unrolls to reveal a labelled pocket for each flag, for easy identification.

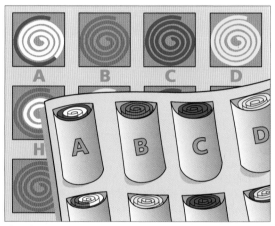

Fig 5 Flag storage.

Halyards and blocks

A flag hoisted on a staff should not be set too low because of slack knots and fittings, nor be so tightly hoisted that the bunting (cloth) is forced into the block (Fig 6). A well-designed ensign staff has a sheave and its own cleat on the staff. Hoist it up tight so knots or fittings are hard against the block. Pull the lower part of the halyard tight so that the hoist does not sag away from the staff. On yards, crosstrees or spreaders, sheaves are not suitable. There should be a hanging block, a simple thimble, or an 'eye'. The latter is probably meant for attaching a block, but a light flag halyard can be threaded through it. There

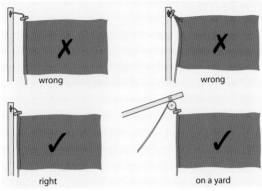

wrong

wrong

right

on a yard

Fig 6 Too loose, too tight.

is no need for flag halyard blocks to be oversize, they only need to be large enough for the flag halyard.

Shoreside

The usual design for a shoreside flag mast is a vertical mast with a lighter topmast. It also has a yard or gaff projecting from two-thirds of its height: this takes the maritime ensign (which in many cases is also the national flag). Crosstrees are at right angles to the plane of this yard and may well have a number of halyard blocks for flags and signals. The head of the topmast has a block suitable for a burgee or house pennant.

Guarding against vandalism

Vandalism is a potential menace to flags ashore. One method for anti-vandalism is shown in Fig 7).

■ The halyard is internal, starting at the bottom with a plate, which can be locked and unlocked, and then travelling up to the sheave at the masthead.

■ The lower corner of the flag is attached to a loop with a weight. This loop slides around and up the mast.

Securing flags

- With the upper corner of the flag attached, it is hauled up by access to the lockable plate. The weighted loop keeps the flag in position and taut.

- Once it is hoisted, the halyard is cleated off inside the hollow pole and the access door is locked. There is now no external halyard for anyone to climb or to disturb and this works quite well.

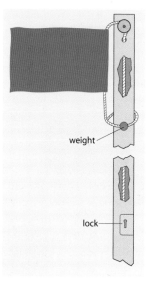

Fig 7 Anti-vandal device.

Some countries, like the UK, have a national flag, *and* a civil or maritime ensign, *and* a naval ensign. The national flag is flown on shore, the civil or maritime ensign is flown by the merchant navy and ordinary yachtsmen, and the naval ensign is reserved for the navy. The maritime ensign therefore is not automatically a replica of the national flag (see page 20). In the UK, for instance, the national flag is the Union flag, and is only flown ashore or on Her Majesty's ships, but the general maritime ensign has the Union flag in the canton and a red field.

Generally, countries with specific ensigns, as opposed to just one national flag, retain their country's identity in the canton but they have different coloured fields. They then have badges or symbols (defacements) for individual or government institutitons. Ireland, for instance, an independent republic, has inherited some of the same customs, placing the national flag in the canton, and defacing a blue field for a yacht club ensign (Fig 8).

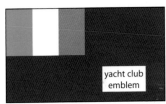

Fig 8 Ireland – yacht club ensign.

There is a legal requirement for most vessels to have an ensign, and to display it at all the correct times. Rules exist as to where it is worn because its position signifies that the flag in question is indeed an ensign. Flags other than ensigns may not be worn in an ensign position. All leading maritime nations have rules about their own ensigns, however the 184 countries who are signatories to the United Nations Convention on the Law of the Sea (UNCLOS 1982) will be governed by this convention (see Flags and the law, page 75).

Ensigns

Basic UK ensigns

These are white, blue, and red (see Fig 9). That is to say that they have the Union flag in the canton and the fields are white, blue or red. The white ensign showing St George's cross is only flown by ships of the British Navy and members of the Royal Yacht Squadron, which is the world's oldest and the most senior British yacht club.

Naval ensign (White ensign)

Blue ensign

Civil ensign (Red ensign)

UK Border Agency ensign

Fig 9 Some British ensigns.

The (undefaced) blue ensign may be flown on merchant ships where the captain is a member of the naval reserve, on auxiliary naval vessels, on certain govrnment vessels, or used by selected yacht clubs (see Appendix 1).

The red ensign (undefaced) is the British merchant ensign and may be, or must be, flown without any special permit on all British ships (see Flags and the law, page 75).

Coastguard ensign

Ships in the service of the Government

Fig 10 More British government ensigns.

FORMER UK COLONIES AND THE COMMONWEALTH

There are numerous flags around the world with the British Union flag in the upper canton (Fig 11). This is a legacy of the British empire, but many remain in countries which have since become independent. Yacht clubs in places which were then colonies were granted warrants for blue and defaced ensigns, in exactly the same way as clubs in Great Britain. Some of these yacht clubs have retained their royal warrants and defaced ensigns after independence. Below are two ensigns from islands that are closely aligned with New Zealand. In 2015 and 2016 New Zealand voted not to change their flag, which has the Union flag in the canton. As 'freely associated states', Niue and the Cook Islands are members of the Commonwealth, and have retained the Union flag in their ensigns.

Fig 11 Commonwealth ensigns retaining the Union flag: Cook Islands and Niue.

BRITISH GOVERNMENT ENSIGNS

There are 25 blue ensigns defaced by badges, logos, crowns, etc. These may be flown by vessels and shore bases of nominated government departments and officially recognised bodies (Fig 12). There are seven defaced red ensigns of this sort, Trinity House having one of them. There is no special reason why one organisation has blue and another red. These organisations may or may not also fly their own institutional flags, but defaced ensigns obey the normal ensign rules. Yacht clubs are not included in this category.

Fig 12 Ensigns of the Commissioners of Northern Lights and the Commissioners of Irish Lights.

Ensigns

Special ensigns and yacht club special ensigns

There are special ensigns from the UK, Scandinavian countries, the Netherlands and elsewhere. These ensigns are only to be used with permission to the individual person or his appointment/function.

In the case of the UK there is a confusing array of special ensigns. Various members of specific yacht clubs may fly defaced red, blue or defaced blue ensigns or a white ensign providing they have been granted an Admiralty warrant. (See Appendix for specific yacht clubs.) In the UK this is granted by the Secretary of Defence on behalf of the monarch. There is no correlation between the holding of an Admiralty warrant for a special ensign and having 'royal' in the title of the club. There are 'royal' clubs with and without ensign warrants, there are non-royal clubs with ensign warrants. Whether an ensign is red defaced or blue defaced has no significance.

- ▪ Yacht club special ensigns may not be flown unless the respective and corresponding burgee, or flag officer's flag, is flying as well.
- ▪ A special ensign applies to a particular owner on a particular yacht. Sailing on a yacht other than his own does not give him the right to fly his special ensign.
- ▪ In the UK and its dependencies, misuse of ensigns can attract a considerable fine.
- ▪ Owners who do fly a special ensign need to be more observant of the etiquette surrounding them.

Fig 12a Ensigns and House Flag of National Historic Ships.

Anguilla

Bermuda

British Virgin Islands

British Indian Ocean Territory

Fig 13 Ensigns of overseas territories.

Unlike the special ensigns of government bodies, etc (Fig 10), the yacht club ensign may only be hoisted when the club burgee is flying. The rule is inflexible. Therefore unlike the practice with the US ensign (see page 35), the burgee must be hoisted first before the ensign and the ensign lowered prior to the burgee. Other distinct rules surround the use of the yacht club ensign:

Ensigns – Superiority

- A warrant is granted to an individual yacht and owner in the respective club: only then may the owner fly the special ensign.
- On disposal of that particular yacht, the warrant ceases.
- A warrant cannot be issued for houseboats, etc; the vessel must be genuinely cruising.
- If there are joint owners all must be eligible for the same ensign.

Superiority of ensigns

The unofficial order of superiority for ensigns among yacht clubs is as follows:

- White
- Undefaced blue
- Defaced blue
- Defaced red
- Red

Fig 14 Defaced blue ensign for the Ministry of Defence, Police.

Use on shore

The red ensign may be used on shore, though the general public in Britain would consider it as 'the merchant navy flag'. The white and blue ensigns are maritime flags and their use on shore is usually incorrect. However, there are exceptions. Warranted ensigns may be flown at shore stations of the establishment to which they belong. They must not be flown at the head of a flagpole but should be flown from a yardarm. In an urban setting, a flagpole that comes out obliquely from a building seems acceptable. The white ensign is used at naval establishments. Both may be used for decoration during national festivals (jubilees, war anniversaries etc), if they are 'hung out', suspended on a line or part of a set of small flags.

Courtesy flags

The ensign also has a role as a courtesy flag, however it is often misunderstood. Its primary function is to indicate to a foreign country that you are a visitor and that you recognise, and agree to abide by, the laws of that country whilst you are there. It is a way of indicating a token of respect and an acknowledgement that you are a guest in their country.

You should raise it once within 12M of a foreign shore, unless you require Customs clearance. See Q flag, page 74.

Courtesy flags are not really meant to indicate the nationality of those on board since the ensign will declare your country of origin, however see the 'Charterer's ensign' section for an unofficial practice which has been adopted amongst charter fleets.

Ensigns

- If the country has no separate maritime ensign, then you show a smaller version of the national flag.
- The courtesy ensign is usually about one third or one half bigger than a signal flag. It should be clean, in good condition and not ridiculously small. An overly small flag could be interpreted as being insulting.
- It should be flown from a senior position in the vessel: on a forward mast on ships, from the starboard spreader on yachts. The powerboat equivalent is above any other signals there.
- Yachts engaged in racing do not need to keep the courtesy flag up, but it should be rehoisted after they have crossed the finishing line.

Between some European countries, for instance for yachts in and out of Baltic ports, where a different nation is visited each day, there is some slackness, but it is incorrect not to fly a courtesy flag. EU flags have nothing to do with it and do not affect the rules.

In some countries not flying a courtesy flag is an offence. There are also laws about disrespect to the flag, which include it being torn or dirty. You should check a country's laws on its flags before you arrive (see also Flags and the law, page 75).

Local regional flags may be an additional option, but are not a substitute. A British boat in a port in Brittany *must* have the French *Tricolore* in the starboard spreaders and she *may care* to hoist the black and white flag of Brittany in an inferior position, ie below the *Tricolore*, or on the port spreader.

The Welsh dragon, St Andrew's cross, St George's cross and St Patrick's cross are all primarily land flags and not for use by cruising sailors. See St George's flag, page 20, for its exceptional use at sea. Nevertheless they can be seen on yachts, often declaring the proud origins of their owners, or by visitors using them (incorrectly) as courtesy flags.

FOREIGN YACHTS VISITING OTHER COUNTRIES

Foreign yachts visiting other countries should fly their own ensigns at the rear of their vessels, and a smaller (but not offensively miniscule) version of the flag of the country being visited (host country) should be hoisted up tight and flying nicely in the starboard spreaders. Foreign yachts visiting the UK should use a small version of the red maritime ensign and not the British Union flag.

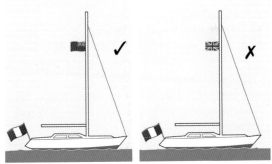

Fig 15a Yachts visiting the UK should fly a small version of the British red ensign not the Union flag. A British yacht visiting a foreign country such as Italy or Germany would fly the Italian or German national flag at the starboard spreaders.

Fig 15b A British yacht visiting Germany.

Ensign of charterer

The custom has arisen for yachts on charter to show an ensign of the charterer's nationality when this nationality is different from the ensign nationality of the vessel. So, a Malaysian owned and registered yacht with an Australian charter party on board will wear the Australian ensign in the rigging and the Malaysian ensign at the ensign staff aft. If she then visits Thailand, she must hoist the Thai courtesy ensign, and not offend her host country. So:

- The Malaysian ensign will be at the stern.
- The Thai ensign at starboard spreader.
- Australian ensign is placed at a position inferior to the Thai courtesy flag, either beneath it or else on the port spreader.

If the charterers are of several nationalities, no more flags should be hoisted and it is probably best to forget the charter ensign!

International ensigns

Examples of nationalities and regions are given below in alphabetical order.

BELGIUM

Belgian ensigns are rectangular, approaching a square (proportion 2:3). The national flag and ensign for vessels in general is the black, yellow and red *Tricolore* (Fig 16). The state ensign has a crown and lion on the yellow. Specified yacht clubs, including the Royal Belgian Yacht Club of Belgium, the Royal Motor Yacht Club of Belgium and the North Sea Yacht Club, with warrants, have a Belgian crown.

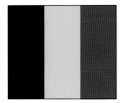

Maritime ensign

Yacht ensign (warranted clubs)

Fig 16 Belgium – ensign and yacht ensign.

DENMARK

Denmark has several ensigns. Most ships show the Danish national white cross on red as the ensign, but the state ensign and naval ensign are the same, only swallow-tailed (Fig 17). A further state ensign has a Danish crown in the top canton of the swallow-tailed flag and is also carried by the royal yacht. The Royal Danish Yacht Club has the swallowtail ensign defaced by the crown, and three stars in the top canton.

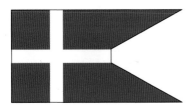

State and naval ensign

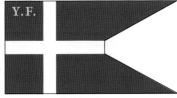

Yacht ensign

Fig 17 Denmark.

Ensigns – International

EUROPEAN UNION

The EU (European Union) flag is not an ensign, but it is often seen with French, Dutch, German (see Fig 18), etc national ensigns in the canton. The fly is made up of the EU ring of stars on a blue field. However this flag is not an ensign and has no meaning.

Fig 18 European Union flag with German national colours (no status).

FINLAND

Finland has the same merchant ensign as her national flag (Fig 19). There is a distinct naval ensign: swallow-tailed and defaced; a state ensign, defaced; a yacht ensign; and a yacht club commodore burgee. The Finnish Åland Islands follow a similar system, but the yacht ensign is swallow-tailed in island colours.

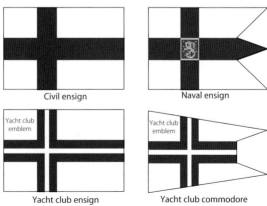

Civil ensign

Naval ensign

Yacht club emblem

Yacht club ensign

Yacht club emblem

Yacht club commodore

Fig 19 Finland.

FRANCE

France has a subtle difference between land and sea for its famous blue, white and red *Tricolore*. On land the stripes are of equal thickness; at sea the thickness from the hoist is 90:99:111; this is said to counteract perspective at a distance. This sea flag is also the jack. The Yacht Club de France has a single white star on the blue of the ensign and a blue star on the white (nothing on the red).

Fig 20 The French ensign and the ensign of the Yacht Club de France.

Ensigns – International

JAPAN

The national flag and maritime ensign is a red disc on white, but the naval ensign is a smaller red disc with rays from it alternating red and white (Fig 21). This is used by authorised yacht clubs. Other yacht clubs are allocated an undefaced blue ensign with the national flag, plain red sun on white, in the upper canton. The national flag is also the jack. This is similar to the British 'system'.

National flag and maritime ensign

Naval ensign

Japan Sailing Federation

Fig 21 Japanese ensigns.

NETHERLANDS

The tricolour red, white and blue of equal horizontal stripes serves as both national flag and ensign, but there are some defaced special ensigns (Fig 22). The ensign is defaced by crown and fouled anchor for merchant ships commanded by naval reserve officers (cf British blue ensign). Some senior yacht clubs have defaced ensigns, such as the Royal Maas which has its burgee design reappearing in the top canton of the national ensign; and the Royal Netherlands in the centre of the white band. The navy has the national colours in a spiral effect as a jack and there is also a civil jack for optional use which has a slight variation on this design.

Ensign

Royal Dutch Sailing and Rowing
Club ensign

Fig 22 Netherlands ensigns.

Ensigns – International

NORWAY

The national flag is also the general ensign (Fig 23). The naval ensign is a triple swallowtail. The customs ensign is the naval ensign defaced in the centre. Selected yacht clubs, including KDY, the Royal Norwegian Yacht Club, have the naval ensign with small defacements in the centre of the cross: the crown with initials, or symbol of the respective club.

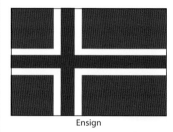

Ensign

Ensign of warranted clubs
(defacement varies)

Fig 23 Norwegian ensigns.

REGIONAL FLAGS

Countries with regional areas and identities within them such as Catalonia, Brittany, Lapland, Wales and Scotland, etc have their own flags. However these are not ensigns and should never be flown in ensign positions. They are often offered as courtesy ensigns in the courtesy flag position. However, see page 26.

SPAIN

With ensigns for Customs and yacht clubs, Spain also has a jack as well as its national flag and ensign (Fig 24). The Spanish flag and ensign has the royal arms of Spanish union (Castile, Aragon, etc) upon it, but a version without it counts as a civil ensign. Customs has one of these ensigns defaced. Selected yacht clubs are permitted an ensign with a large blue Spanish crown in the centre of the flag. The colours are in the ratio of 5:10:5.

National flag

Yacht club ensign

Fig 24 Spanish ensigns.

UNITED STATES OF AMERICA

The national flag and naval ensign are the same (Fig 26). It commands, and receives, particular respect. There are rules for the flag at sea and ashore. It can fly from a yardarm on shore and be physically below a burgee or special flag, because the yard represents the yard of a ship. It may be at the head of a vertical flagpole on shore. When on US territory it must be higher, or equal to, others.

Ensigns – International

Fig 25 Ensign of USA.

It is also known as: the Stars and Stripes, Star Spangled Banner or Old Glory. The pattern of stripes dates back to the 17th century (British) East India Company, though the 13 alternate red and white stripes representing the original 13 colonies or states have been in position since 1776. See A Short History (page 1) for further details.

Fig 26 Yacht ensign

Fig 27 Power Squadron flag

Betsy Ross

There is a second ensign for US vessels. This is the yacht ensign (Fig 27), known as the Betsy Ross, which has a fouled anchor in the canton. It is permissible for any recreational craft to wear the yacht ensign. The yacht owner does not have to belong to a club or have a permit to use it. However it is only permissible within the waters of the United States (see Flags and the law, page 75).

On a ship or yacht the US ensign is hoisted at morning colours and lowered at evening colours, or when all the crew leave the vessel. It is hoisted before all other flags and lowered after them. (This differs from some UK yacht clubs.) It is worn from an ensign staff on the stern and the US practice is to show a conspicuously large ensign on any vessel but it is incorrect for the flag to touch the water. Just a reminder here that the US jack (see page 38) is a blue flag with the fifty white stars only and is flown from a jackstaff. There are certain occasions for this and the jack will not be flown on the jackstaff without the Stars and Stripes on the ensign staff. The rules for the Stars and Stripes on land are numerous and do not necessarily apply at sea or on ships. The US ensign may be flown upside down to indicate distress, and it would be recognised as such in US waters but probably not abroad. Upside down ensigns are not internationally adopted as a signal of distress because many national flags, such as those with vertical stripes, look exactly the same when inverted.

Only ensigns are used for dipping (salutes) and half-masted for deaths of national and international figures, owner of the vessel, person in company, club or institution.

Unofficial indicator of distress in US waters only

Jacks

The term jack refers to the small flag worn on a staff at the bows. The position defines the flag, so it is not a jack if worn anywhere else. Originally it was hoisted on the foremost spar (the topmast of the sprit). When these spars were no longer used the jack was moved to a staff at the bows, which became the jack staff.

Like many flag traditions the pilot or civil jack dates back to the days of sailing warships. It was also flown by merchants requiring a pilot.

These days a jack is seldom used except on naval ships who wear the Union flag when not under way, and not in a repair dock. It is then called the Union Jack, which is the name often given, erroneously, to the British national flag. British non-naval vessels, such as private yachts, sail or power, may wear a 'pilot jack', which is the Union flag with a white border, when the vessel is alongside, or when it is on a mooring or anchored, during the same hours, and in conjunction with, the ensign. Whilst they can be flown, broadly speaking, when the yacht's owner's mood takes them, according to the etiquette above, they are usually flown to add a bit of colour for a special event, such as a yacht club muster.

Fig 28 USA jack.

Fig 29 Dutch civil jack.

Warships of the US wear a blue flag with 50 white stars on a jackstaff. This is the same as the canton of the US national flag. Other nations' navies may fly various jacks: the Dutch are particularly keen on theirs. Occasionally ships and yachts may fly a flag from a jackstaff, but this would be of a trade or house nature and is not a jack merely because it is on the jackstaff.

Fig 30 First Navy jack.

After the bombing of the World Trade Center towers in New York the US navy reintroduced the occasional use of their First Navy Jack, which some sources date from 1775, showing a rattlesnake and the phrase DONT TREAD ON ME (*sic*) which naval ships fly as and when directed.

The history of the UK Union flag

When James VI of Scotland became King James I of England, he created a new flag to symbolise the united thrones. The English red cross of St George was combined with the Scottish white cross of St Andrew. Later the Union flag became even more complex when the St Patrick's cross of red diagonals on white was added to celebrate the Act of Union with Ireland.

Fig 31 British pilot jack.

Jacks

- Ships of the British Royal Navy, (and only the navy) fly the Union flag as a jack when in harbour or at anchor between colours (sunrise to sunset), or when the ship is dressed overall.
- They will fly it at the masthead (not on the jackstaff) when they have on board the following people:
  - ❑ an Admiral of the Fleet (very few left and a rank which is currently in abeyance);
  - ❑ the First Sea Lord;
  - ❑ former First Sea Lords;
  - ❑ and Admirals who are, or have been, Chief of Defence Staff.
- Naval vessels will fly it at the peak, or on the yardarm, when they are conducting a court martial.
- No other vessel is allowed to fly the Union flag, and it falls under the penalties for carrying improper colours. (See the section on Law)
- British (non-naval) ships may wear a *pilot jack*, which is the Union flag with a white border: It can be worn when dressed overall or at anchor or alongside. It is not normally flown under way.

The yacht club burgee is the primary flag for most sailing clubs, or associations. The conventional yacht burgee is triangular and usually flown from the head of the main mast. With the proliferation of masthead electronics and other equipment, clubs have been obliged to allow their burgees to be flown at the starboard spreader. This is not entirely satisfactory because other flags may be required at this position and it is often obscured when the sails are hoisted. On dinghies and launches, the burgee may be displayed as a badge on each bow. On a powerboat without any form of mast, the burgee may be worn on a jackstaff on the stemhead. This does not make it a jack and the practice is rare. A few clubs rule that their members may only fly their burgee at the masthead and they forbid other positions.

Burgee facts

■ The burgee is a central symbol of the club and will be seen on the masthead of the flagpoles of yacht clubs, whether on a waterfront or in a city. It is also likely to be painted on the front door, printed on stationery, trophies, etc.

■ A burgee worn on a sailing yacht indicates that it is not racing. If a yacht is racing, the burgee should not be flying.

■ A yachtsman sailing someone else's boat will fly his own club burgee. However, if the owner is in effective control but not actually on board, then his burgee can be worn, eg if the boat is out for a day trip with friends of the owner.

It is generally considered incorrect to fly two yacht club burgees at the same time, This is called being 'double flagged' and some yacht clubs positively forbid it. If you (owner or skipper) belong to more than one club you should fly the burgee of the club whose event you are attending and your member's flag of the second club in an inferior position. See membership flags, page 40, and be guided by your clubs' rules.

Burgees

Mounting a burgee on a cane

The yacht club burgee is hoisted to the masthead on a shoreside mast or on a powered vessel. Ideally it should be at the masthead on sailing yachts but many yacht clubs accept it at the starboard spreaders, see Fig 62.

The edict from certain yacht clubs that their burgee must be flown from the masthead ('*at the truck*') however, poses a dilemma. Most yachts have VHF aerials and wind instruments which must not be imperilled. VHF aerials are about 1m long. So you need to set the burgee away from it in such a way that when streaming out horizontally it will clear the aerial, and it has to be sufficiently high that it will clear all instrumentation when drooping ('*at the droop*').

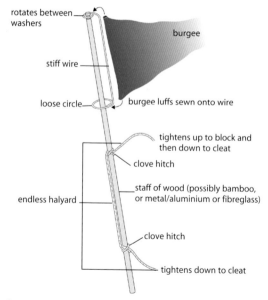

rotates between washers

burgee

stiff wire

loose circle

burgee luffs sewn onto wire

tightens up to block and then down to cleat

clove hitch

staff of wood (possibly bamboo, or metal/aluminium or fibreglass)

endless halyard

clove hitch

tightens down to cleat

Fig 32 How to make a burgee fly true and clear: each burgee needs its own pole.

The only answer is to mount your burgee on a fairly stiff long cane, metal tube or fibreglass rod, (known as a *pig stick* in the USA). The editor has a 2.4m (8ft) fibreglass rod with a swivel set in the top, see Fig 32. The washers at the top and circular loop in the wire at the bottom allow it to rotate freely.

Some people simply stitch their burgee onto a bamboo garden cane but if the flag can't swivel it will not fly freely. Sometimes burgees come with a toggle and a line stitched into the hoist. You can lash the toggle to the top section of the bent wire and tension the bottom of the line to the metal loop at the bottom, as long as you don't impede the swivelling action. Alternatively you can stitch the burgee more permanently onto the wire, or remove the line and toggle, open the wire, and feed the hoist of the burgee up the shank and then re-bend the wire. You can then secure it with a bit of stitching. However the wire might not be very malleable, and this permanent arrangement means that you will need a second cane for a different burgee, so it is a less flexible set up. The 'droop' can still cause a problem if your cane isn't long enough to allow your burgee to fly sufficiently high for it to clear all the instruments at the droop. The Dutch in particular use long pennants at their mastheads. In order to reduce the 'droop' they have an extrusion at 90° from their swivel to support the top edge of the flag. You can stitch the flag along the section of the extrusion. This greatly reduces the droop and particularly helps the flag to fly nicely in light airs. See Fig 33.

Securing a masthead burgee

You now have to get this arrangement flying at the masthead. There are a couple of ways of achieving this. One is to have a small cheek-block riveted onto the less cluttered side of the mast. See Fig 33. Reeve a thin line, usually 4mm, pre-stretched, line through it and tie the ends together to make it endless. Set a pair of hitches on the cane below the halfway point in order to acquire adequate clearance above the mast truck. You need

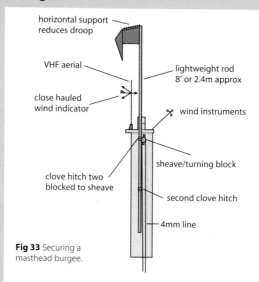

horizontal support reduces droop

VHF aerial

lightweight rod 8' or 2.4m approx

close hauled wind indicator

wind instruments

sheave/turning block

clove hitch two blocked to sheave

second clove hitch

4mm line

Fig 33 Securing a masthead burgee.

a reasonable space and good tension between the hitches. The lower hitch needs to be quite near the bottom of the cane in order to provide good control over the lower end.

This is a matter of trial and error and once happy with the set of your flag you should probably mark the pole for future reference. Hoisting this paraphernalia and keeping the capsized cane clear of the rigging on the way up is easier said than done, particularly on a windy day. Standing on the side-deck and guiding it away from the mast will help. Once you have got the top hitch close-up to the block you heave down tight on the downhaul side of the line and with any luck the staff and flag should become erect. You can then tie it off somewhere at the base of the mast. You need quite a lot of tension on both sides of this continuous line to prevent it from sagging. The advantage of this system is that you do not permanently extend your mast height.

One alternative is to have a curved staff (see Fig 34) riveted onto the mast with a pair of tabs, as a permanent arrangement. It needs an eyelet on the outboard end from which you suspend a small block, and you reeve your halyard through that. You then raise your burgee on its cane and two-block the top hitch to the block and tension up both sides of the line as above. The bend on the staff takes the flag away from the instruments but the cane doesn't have the mast to lie against and therefore is slightly more difficult to keep truly vertical. Some people feel that burgees look better flying directly above the mast rather than slightly off to one

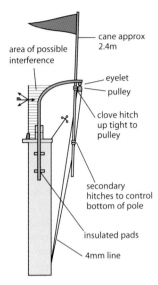

cane approx 2.4m

area of possible interference

eyelet
pulley

clove hitch up tight to pulley

secondary hitches to control bottom of pole

insulated pads

4mm line

Fig 34 Securing a burgee on a rod with a swept bend.

side, but it is an easier place to which to raise the cane and reduces the risk of clobbering the instruments on the way up. So it is an acceptable alternative. The only issue with this system is that when your mast is ashore, or in a mast rack, the curved rod may be less easy to accommodate.

Straight or curved, hoisting your bamboo or fibreglass burgee cane to the eyelet will give a great deal more height for clearance above your aerial, but remains removable for bridge clearances.

There is a caveat to adding metal rods to the masthead, however. Mounting a parallel metal rod on the mast makes it act as an extension of the 'earth'. Mounting it near an aerial runs the risk that it may resonate and divert the VHF and AIS signals away from the aerial. This particularly risks jeopardising the 'gain' in AIS signals. Class B AIS, used by most yachts only transmits

Burgees

at 0.5W, whereas the VHF voice channels transmit at 25W. Therefore any degradation in the AIS signal (often sharing the VHF coaxial cable via a splitter) is much more critical. Any metal rod fixed to the mast head should be insulated and modest. Canes of fibreglass, bamboo or a non-conductive material should then be used for any further height required.

Advice from the National Marine Electronics Association (NMEA) is that ideally any metal rod should be at least 2m horizontally and 2m vertically away from an aerial. Furthermore the rod should not be projecting into an aerial's 360° field of view. On many yachts this almost impossible to achieve. So the relatively modest stainless, insulated rod rivetted to the masthead, but below the top of the aerial is a compromise approach. The further height still required is achieved with the burgee cane as described above. If you do add a metal rod to your masthead and you notice your AIS performance is diminished then you may have to rethink your burgee arrangement.

Having finally got this assemblage flying proudly erect many skippers are reluctant to go through this exercise more often than strictly necessary. Luckily most yacht clubs expect their burgees to remain aloft whilst the vessel is in commission and the member is in effective control. This means it can stay up at night, at sea or in harbour. A lashing with which you can pull the halyard clear of the mast, and tie it off to a shroud should help to prevent frapping in strong winds.

Crowns on burgees

Yacht clubs with royal patronage have crowns on their burgees, and/or their ensigns. The British crowns do not necessarily change with each monarch, but they are changed if the new monarch specifically instructs that he/she wants it changed. The current Saint Edward's crown replaced the old imperial crown in 1952 on the instructions of the Queen, when she was crowned, and all British yacht club burgees should have been changed at that time.

Flag officers and club officials

The burgees carried by certain club officials differ from the standard burgee of the club. It is a matter for each club's rules whether this is the case, but there is a general usage in Great Britain and those countries which follow its systems. In many countries the president of a yacht club is called the commo-

Burgee

dore, who may be supported by a vice commodore and rear commodore (Fig 36). In Europe, each club has a president and subsidiary officials to that title. Commodores, etc, are described as *flag officers* (even if they never fly a flag, but this follows naval parlance).

Fig 35 Burgee of the Royal Western Yacht Club.

Some clubs appoint an admiral, president, or some distinguished person who ranks above the commodore, but who does not take part in the day-to-day workings of the club. The usual burgee for him or her is the design of the club burgee but on a rectangular flag. Whether one calls this a burgee or a flag is uncertain! All these special burgees follow the same hoisting and flying rules as the club burgee for a member.

There may be further club officials with flags or burgees. One seen occasionally is a 'past commodore' flag either worn at the masthead as a burgee or additional to the club burgee from a spreader; designs for this vary. Occasionally other one-off

Admiral

Commodore

Fig 36 Royal Western Yacht club officers' burgees.

burgees/flags exist for captains of racing or cruising but these will not be found in a reference of standard club burgees and it is likely that only their own club members will know what they mean.

In the UK, the Royal London YC and others allow boats and tenders 'which can conveniently be hoisted on board a yacht' to wear the same special ensign; presumably the burgee would be at the bow. This club unusually allows other club burgees to be flown simultaneously with its own, but only on a second or even third mast. The Royal Western YC specifies that no special

Burgee variations

The Royal Canadian Yacht Club follows neither the British nor the US burgee system for flag officers. The committee decided that whilst it would have been logical to emulate the English custom of using balls in the hoist to denote rank, the club already had devices in the hoist. These were (and remain) a crown in the upper hoist and a beaver in the lower hoist. The committee therefore decided to use changes of colour instead. The club burgee is pennant shaped. The patron has the same design in a rectangular flag. The commodore and vice commodore have swallow-tailed burgees, but in this Canadian system they have small alterations to the ordinary burgee design. The commodore also has an alternative tapering swallowtail.

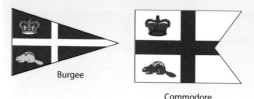

Fig 37 The members' (left) and Commodore's burgee of the Royal Canadian Yacht Club.

ensign should be flown unless the burgee is at the masthead; other clubs have a similar rule (only one club burgee at a time).

Membership flag

As mentioned, it is nearly always incorrect to show burgees of more than one club at a time. To overcome this some clubs have a membership flag (Fig 39). This is rectangular and usually a slight variation on the club burgee design.

It can be hoisted to a spreader if you have the burgee of another club at the masthead (see page 41). In reality, not many members possess them. Individual club rules may allocate additional special meanings, as set out in respective club rules. For instance, at least one club decrees that if the membership flag is hoisted with its own club burgee aloft, it is said to mean 'members of our club, do come aboard'!

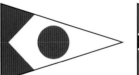 

Fig 38 Burgees of the Cruising Association and the Royal Lymington Yacht Club.

Cruising Association
membership flag

Royal Lymington Yacht Club
membership flag

Fig 39 Some clubs and associations have membership flags in addition to regular burgees.

Burgees

United States flag officers

In the US and countries that follow their yachting customs, the system for burgees/flags of club flag officers is totally different from that described above. Instead of a defaced club burgee, there is a uniform system of specific signals to denote flag rank. Four are widely recognised and officially lodged with the Congress of the United States, they are: commodore, vice commodore, rear commodore and fleet captain (Fig 40).

Unlike the British and Canadian flag officers, the eligible yacht owners only fly these flag officer flags at club events and at the club's location. At other times and places the flag officers simply fly the club burgee like any other member. Across the vast waterways of the United States, there are undoubtedly variations and there are some that are rather like the Royal Canadian YC system. They may well also have small stars to designate rank.

Such stars occur in an alternative system currently used by the New York Yacht Club (Fig 41). The higher the rank the more

Yacht club commodore

Yacht club vice commodore

Yacht club rear commodore

Yacht fleet captain

Fig 40 United States flag officers.

stars they have. This is the reverse of the British system, where the higher the rank the fewer discs on their flags. The club has a standard race committee flag, blue with a red fouled anchor and white letters 'RC'. This is common to many US clubs.

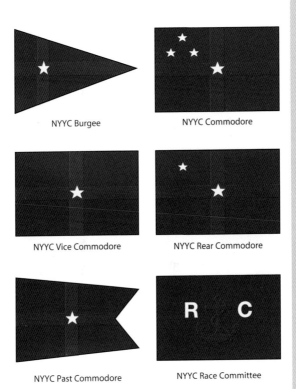

NYYC Burgee

NYYC Commodore

NYYC Vice Commodore

NYYC Rear Commodore

NYYC Past Commodore

NYYC Race Committee

Fig 41 New York Yacht Club flag officers.

Other flags

House flag

This usually means the private signal of a shipping company and is worn at the masthead of a merchant ship. It is sometimes a rectangle, sometimes swallow-tailed. It may be on large freighters or cruise ships, but it can also be seen on local work boats, dredgers, and specialised ships. It may represent the company logo but it is still known as a house flag. There may be a corresponding marking on a funnel. It may also be the personal flag of the owner. There are no rules for design, other than avoiding existing patterns.

It is usually worn by the ship/yacht when in harbour, temporarily in dock, and when the owner is on board. However, commercial shipping lines are inclined to leave theirs flying at sea. It should be flown in an inferior position to any courtesy flags or ensigns (Fig 42).

Cunard   P & O Line

Fig 42 House flags.

Private signal or owner's flag

This is the yachtsman's equivalent to the house flag, but not often seen. Another name for it is the *owner's* flag. It can be any reasonable shape but is usually rectangular or nearly square. In the US the swallowtail shape is traditional. Any design that does not clash with any existing flags is acceptable but initials are not usually used. The flag is worn on a 'subsidiary mast': a second mast on a motor yacht, the foremast of a schooner, or lower down in the rigging. It should not be at the main masthead (though, as stated, this is customary for house flags on commercial shipping), which is reserved for the yacht club burgee. The private signal is not worn by the yacht unless the owner is on board, or effectively based there, visiting a nearby vessel, or ashore locally. Some yacht clubs have a rule which states that when the club burgee is flying, then no private signal may be shown; see the individual club's rules.

H L Brookes

Stanley Woodward Jr

Fig 43 Private signals.

Builder's flag

For commercial craft, warships or yachts, the builder of the vessel may fly his own flag before handing over to the owner. It is a variation of the house flag or private signal. The builder will fly it when the vessel is under way, for instance during sea trials, and until the owner takes possession. Once the owner takes over, the builder's flag should be removed.

Racing flag

The racing flag was similar to a private signal. They are rare these days but can be seen in old photographs on the club wall; and some racing classes may still use them under their own rules.

Previous yacht racing rules demanded that when a yacht was engaged in a race a rectangular or square flag was shown at the sailing yacht's main masthead (Fig 44). It was the same design as the owner's private signal and therefore identified the owner. It also declared that the yacht was racing, thus affecting her conduct on the water. As soon as the boat finished racing, the square flag was lowered and replaced with the burgee. A board with the designs of the flags was displayed on shore during the race.

Once yachts had sails with numbers for identification the racing flag was no longer needed except to indicate the wind angle. With the advent of electronic wind instruments it has become obsolete except on craft without instrumentation. Racing dinghies still occasionally have very lightweight little square flags at their mastheads.

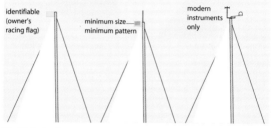

identifiable (owner's racing flag)

minimum size—minimum pattern

modern instruments only

Fig 44 Racing flags.

Prize flag

Racing crews hoisted a replica, though possibly a smaller version of the racing flag for each event in the season that had been a first place, so that a 'string' of them was shown for a yacht that had won several times (Fig 45). They were strung on their own flying halyard from the masthead when not under way. For the even more meticulous show-off, flags of similar size with a figure '2' on blue and '3' on red were part of the string to represent second and third prizes. They were flown at the end of a series or season.

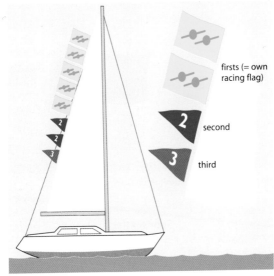

firsts (= own
racing flag)

second

third

Fig 45 Prize flags.

Battle flag

This is a private signal (though never called that) used by racing yachts.

- It is an over-sized flag with a bold design hoisted one third of the way up the forestay of a modern rig when the headsail is not set.
- It is hoisted before or after the actual race, when moving under power, or in harbour. America's Cup boats are often seen flying one when being towed to the starting area of a race.
- It is intended to boost crew morale and a colourful way to intimidate the opposition (Fig 46).
- The shape varies and there may be twin flags, one above the other, the modern substitute for the old racing and prize flags.

Other flags

Fig 46 Battle flag with possible second one.

Sponsor flag

If a regatta or race has a commercial sponsor, they may require competitors to fly a flag with the sponsor's design (Fig 47). This should be quite small as flags are a drag and irritation when racing. It is recommended that it is only flown for the minimum time specified and should be removed as soon as the event has ended. The recent practice of flying sponsors' flags from the backstay is quite incorrect and should be avoided.

Fig 47 Sponsor flag in ensign position.

Association flags

The word 'association' does not represent any one type of yachting institution. If it is in the title of a club-type body with private members, then its flags follow yacht club practice. In the US, classes, racing or production yachts (eg one-designs) may have rectangular or triangular flags. It follows that 'club-type association' burgees cannot be flown with another club burgee, but in the US the class-type association can. In any country which has a national yachting authority, that authority will be a member of World Sailing (formerly ISAF). If that authority has a flag for use on yachts, this can follow the same procedure as class-type association. However, it is usually only flown at some specific rally or celebration day of the authority itself. In Great Britain there is a rectangular flag available from the national yachting authority: the Royal Yachting Association. However, flying it, except in the circumstances just mentioned, is usually meaningless.

Association of Dunkirk Little Ships

The only vessels, apart from ships with admirals on duty, entitled to fly the St George's flag are members of the Association of Dunkirk Little Ships. They may fly the flag from the jackstaff with their Association flag at the masthead when sailing together in company. Anywhere else afloat it is illegal.

Defence and official flags

There are hundreds of special flags afloat for various commanders in numerous countries. These are separate from ensigns and are worn from positions in the middle of the ship. Examples are the French *Capitaine de Vaisseau*, and French Customs (Fig 48). Turkish Customs, for instance, has a red flag, but with a white rectangle in its centre enclosing a crescent and star. An Italian police vessel flies a simple red pennant (burgee) with slim yellow fouled anchor.

France – Navire des Douanes

France – Capitaine de Vaisseau

Fig 48 French defence flags.

In the United States, combinations of stars and fouled anchors satisfy many requirements. These include naval admirals, marine corps generals, admirals and the Coast Guard.

USA – Admiral

USA – Vice Admiral

Fig 49 US defence flags.

In the UK naval admirals fly the St George's cross (the traditional flag of England) at the masthead; a vice admiral has the same with one disc/ball, rear admiral two discs/balls (Fig 50). These are not ensigns, they are flags of office, hence

Great Britain – Admiral

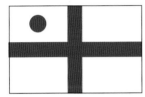

Great Britain – Vice Admiral

Great Britain – Rear Admiral

Fig 50 UK defence flags.

the term 'flag officer'. This is the origin of the British system of yacht club flag officer burgees. When members of the royal family are being conveyed, their launches fly their particular royal standard.

Despite the large number of British maritime organisations, and because of the whole system of ensigns (see page 20) in Great Britain, there are relatively few additional flags for important government organisations on the sea. However, the ancient Corporation of Trinity House which controls light-

Defence and official flags

Fig 51 Trinity House ensign and flag.

houses and seamarks around England and Wales (Fig 51) has an elaborate flag for its Master and its Deputy Master, and a burgee.

The Commissioners of Northern Lights and the Commissioners of Irish Lights also have pennants and burgees (see page 21). These pennants are flown from tenders, working vessels and shore stations. Other notable British flags afloat are those of the Royal National Lifeboat Institution, which also functions throughout Ireland. One complicated but ancient flag is that of the Lord Warden of the Cinque Ports (Fig 52). These five harbours in south-east England were designated specific privileges and duties in the 12th century. Some of these ports have silted up and are no longer accessible by sea and the title has become historic.

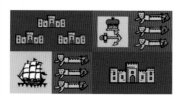

Fig 52 Warden of the Cinque Ports flag.

Code flags

The International Code of Signals (described in detail in the following section) is a set of flags each with a specific meaning. Each sender or recipient can decode the flags in his own language, and arrive at the equivalent text, so this system crosses all language barriers.

They are a distinctive set of coloured flags. There are 26 letters and 10 numerals (0 to 9), three *substitutes* (UK) or *repeaters* (US) and one *answering pennant*. They are rarely used to spell out words, but they are valuable for coded messages. They can then be decoded in the official book of the International Code of Signals. Sailors should familiarise themselves with some of the more important ones.

Semaphore

One system for communication by flags was *semaphore* (Fig 53). Semaphore is now obsolete. Each letter of the alphabet and each numeral, had a unique position for one or both flags. Words were spelt out letter by letter to an observer. However it was a laborious system and has been superceded by the International Code of Signals and modern communications.

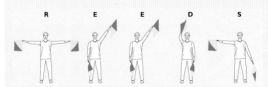

Fig 53 Semaphore.

International Code of Signals

  ANSWERING PENNANT

A – Alfa

I have a diver down: keep well clear at slow speed

B – Bravo

I am taking in, or discharging or carrying dangerous goods

C – Charlie

Yes, affirmative

D – Delta

Keep clear of me: I am manoeuvring with difficulty

E – Echo

I am altering my course to starboard

F – Foxtrot

I am disabled: communicate with me

G – Golf

I require a pilot. *By fishing vessels* I am hauling in nets

H – Hotel

I have a pilot on board

I – India

I am altering my course to port

J – Juliet

I am on fire and have dangerous cargo: keep well clear of me

K – Kilo

I wish to communicate with you

L – Lima

You should stop your vessel instantly

M – Mike

My vessel is stopped and making no way through the water

N – November

No, negative

O – Oscar

Man overboard

P – Papa

Vessel about to put to sea
By fishing vessels My nets are caught fast

International Code of Signals

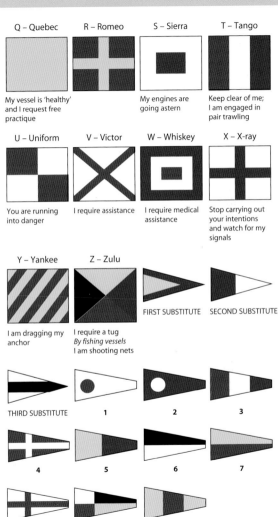

Q – Quebec
My vessel is 'healthy' and I request free practique

R – Romeo

S – Sierra
My engines are going astern

T – Tango
Keep clear of me; I am engaged in pair trawling

U – Uniform
You are running into danger

V – Victor
I require assistance

W – Whiskey
I require medical assistance

X – X-ray
Stop carrying out your intentions and watch for my signals

Y – Yankee
I am dragging my anchor

Z – Zulu
I require a tug
By fishing vessels
I am shooting nets

FIRST SUBSTITUTE

SECOND SUBSTITUTE

THIRD SUBSTITUTE

1

2

3

4

5

6

7

8

9

0

International Code of Signals

The flags must be visible, identifiable, and not too small even if the vessel is small. Some very small flags are sold in yacht chandlers. These are impracticable for passing any kind of message and are mostly sold for decoration (see Dressing ship, pages 92–5)

There are two-, three- and four-flag messages. These can be found in the International Code of Signals, published by the International Maritime Organization (IMO). There are also three Tables of Complements, each of which provides for specific situations such as towing, medical problems, times, dates, positions and bearings, etc. When added to the main code signals they expand the vocabulary to several thousand messages.

In the US there is also an extra flag for 'I have a diver down, please keep clear' (Fig 54). This is a red flag with a diagonal white stripe. It is also commonly seen in the Caribbean, Mediterranean and elsewhere. Nevertheless it is not part of the International Code of Signals and the blue and white 'A' flag for having a diver down has a greater legal status. The code flag T is used in the United States to request a launch service.

Fig 54 Diver down flag (Alfa). Internationally recognised

Diver down flag. Not internationally recognised

Code messages are never more than four flags which is why there are only three substitutes. If there is a series of messages, then the group of flags is hoisted until it has been observed, then another different combination is sent up. In theory (though it is hardly, if ever, used today) there is an order for reading flags by using different positions in the rigging. This is:

- Masthead
- Triatic stay
- Starboard yardarm
- Port yardarm

It is possible that a modern yacht might want two signals at once. If that is the case then the starboard yardarm (or spreader) is always read before the port one.

The three substitute or repeater pennants are available so that a letter or number can be repeated, even though the ship has only a single set of the code. The first substitute repeats the first flag of a group; the second substitute repeats the second; the third repeats the third. So the number 2277 would show as: numeral 2, first sub, numeral 7, third sub (because the first 7 was the third flag in the group). The answering pennant is used to acknowledge a signal, as a decimal point among figures, and for naval ships to indicate that they are using the International Code of Signals and not the naval code of signals.

Yacht only signals

In the US there are long-established conventional yacht signals, that cannot be described as private; yet they do not apply to commercial, or working vessels. Abroad, for instance, in a Caribbean anchorage where there are yachts from a number of nations, other American skippers would probably understand them. They can also be used by foreign yachts in the USA (Fig 55).

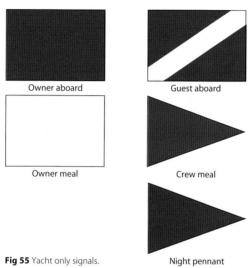

Owner aboard

Guest aboard

Owner meal

Crew meal

Fig 55 Yacht only signals.

Night pennant

These include:

- *Owner absent flag* – the owner is temporarily absent will be back eventually.
- *Guest aboard flag* – there is a guest on board but not the owner.
- *Owner meal flag* – owner eating and visitors not welcome.

These last two signals, though long established, are now optional, while the simple owner absent flag is still recommended.

Navies have their own code flags for signalling. It is not necessary for civilians to be able to read these signals. However, if a naval ship is flying the answering pennant of the International Code, it means that she is using the International Code and expects to be understood by merchant captains and yachtsmen. Yacht racing occasionally makes use of the naval numerals in addition to the International Code numerals. Naval code numerals are rectangular and not pennant shaped (Fig 56). This naval code is standardised for NATO and so applies in the United States, Canada and European member countries of NATO.

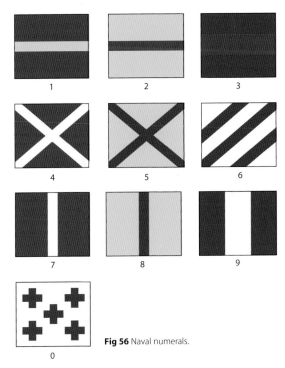

Fig 56 Naval numerals.

Flags used for signalling distress

Electronic communication has immensely improved systems for rescuing people in distress at sea, but there are still flag signals that request help. The definition of distress should be understood. *Distress* is where a boat or person is in imminent danger and requires immediate assistance. Any distress communication has priority over all other messages. *Urgency* is a lesser degree, concerning safety of a boat or a person; for instance a vessel disabled but not sinking, or a medical matter. *Safety* is the third grade and is essentially an alert, for example a navigational or meteorological warning. The flag signals for distress (Fig 57) are:

- The International Code flags NC hoisted one above the other
- Any square flag, any colour, with a ball above or below it

Three single letter signals of Urgency which apply here are:

- **V** I require assistance
- **W** I require medical assistance and safety
- **U** You are running into danger

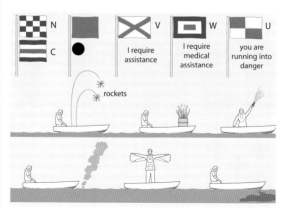

Fig 57 Some visual distress and safety signals at sea.

Answering pennant
'Message understood - I will comply'

N flag
'I am unable to comply'

Fig 57b Replying to air signals

Visual distress signals

Other visual signals for distress are:

- Flashing Morse SOS by light, red parachute or hand-held flares
- Orange smoke
- Repeated slow raising and lowering of arms on each side of the body
- Flames on the vessel (as from a burning oil barrel)
- Orange dye marker in the water
- A piece of orange canvas marked with a black square and circle or appropriate symbol

The last two are for recognition from the air.

Racing code flags

The International Code and other flags have specific meanings in yacht and sailing dinghy racing and are used in conjunction with guns and hooters.

Competitors need to know them, and a general knowledge of them by other vessels will avoid conflict on the water. Races are started and finished from a committee boat, a shore station, or a platform of some sort. The start and finish may not necessarily be in the same place. The finish of an ocean race may be thousands of miles from the start.

Yachts engaged in racing fly:

- Class flags (code flags or numeral pennants or a distinctive house flag) off their backstays
- No burgee
- No ensign after the five minute gun

So if you approach a fleet of yachts flying numeral pennants, code flags, or distinctive identical flags and no ensigns and no burgees, it is a fairly safe bet that they are racing and are best avoided. Whilst they are still bound by the rules of the road they will appreciate the courtesy of being given space. Racing boats will be sailing around tactically while these signals are in use. Look for each end of the starting line, marked by buoys or the committee boat. The committee boat and auxiliary boats running the event may fly a variety of flags. There may be more than one class starting, so a series of starting signals might be on the move: up and down flag halyards. Flags used in controlling races are in Fig 58 and include the answering pennant and substitutes.

Postponement signals

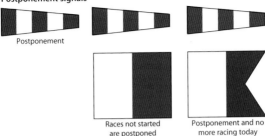

Postponement

Races not started
are postponed

Postponement and no
more racing today

Signals before the start

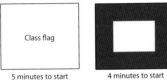

Class flag

5 minutes to start

4 minutes to start
or flag 1 and/or flag Z
or Black flag

Class flag

1 minute to start
Preparatory flag removed

Starting penalties

Round-an-end rule is
in effect

Soft penalty (20%) rule
is in effect

Black flag rule is in
effect

Course change signals

Other signals

Shorten course

Position of next race
mark changed

Collect new instruction
or follow this boat

Fig 58 Flags in yacht and dinghy racing World Sailing signals.

Racing code flags

Abandonment signals

1 hour delay

Postponement of 1–6 hours are indicated by the appropriate numeral pennant

Abandonment
When flown above code flag A or H, indicates that there will be no more racing today

Start and finishing line

Class flag

Start

Start line

Finishing line

Recall signals

All yachts recalled

Individual recall

Protest signals

Time limit for protests is in effect

Mark replacement

Lifejackets must be worn

Boat taking a scoring penalty

There are quite a few reasons for flying flags:

- *Recognition, and a legal requirement* An ensign declares the origin of the vessel, probably indicates the common language on board, and is usually a legal requirement.
- *Authentication* Particular flags represent the river police, Customs, or a local authority.
- *Information and communication* The International Code of Signals is designed to impart meanings that will be understood by all who recognise flags across several languages.
- *Political gestures* Welcoming a head of state (or flag burning).
- *Decoration* Decoration for celebration: yachts *dressed overall* will have crews in a festive mood and it's party time.

The minimal flag display on a vessel depends on the duties or nature of the ship. The obvious minimum is simply the maritime ensign which is a flag flown on a vessel to show its nationality. This applies to all nations. In general, captains and owners are proud to show their nationality. This particularly applies if they are abroad. A working boat at home, such as a dredger, however, is more likely to display signals indicating its function and wear no ensign. Any vessel working in a foreign country should hoist its national ensign. It indicates a possible language difference and the vessel's legal position. Fishing boats are exempt from displaying ensigns.

It used to be common for a yacht in home waters to wear only the yacht club burgee at the masthead. Today it is more likely that there will be no burgee, but there will be an ensign.

Q and courtesy flags

Q flag and courtesy flag

Vessels visiting a foreign country *and requiring customs clearance* should display the yellow Q flag. The Q flag declares 'my vessel is healthy and I request free pratique'. In other words the yacht requires customs clearance so that the crew can come ashore.

Strictly speaking it should go in the position of the courtesy flag until you have cleared Customs because until you are 'cleared in' you have not officially entered the country.

It should be raised as you enter the territorial waters of the country you are visiting, in other words at the point of crossing the 12M limit.

Once you have been cleared you drop the Q flag and replace it with the courtesy flag.

Yachts from European Union member states travelling within the EU will not require customs clearance and therefore have no need to fly the Q flag (see International Code of Signals, page 62).

Legal requirements concerning flags are most likely to apply to the ensign and other national flags. Each country has its own laws. Misuse of flags can invoke fines. In the USA the national flag, which is also the merchant and naval ensign, is still controlled under Acts of Congress. A fairly recent debate was for 'the flag desecration constitutional amendment' which would have made burning the US flag a punishable crime. It was defeated in the Senate.

Merchant Shipping Act

British yachts are treated as merchant vessels and therefore have to comply with the Merchant Shipping Act which was amended in 1995. Certain ensigns afloat were regulated by the Merchant Shipping Act of 1894. The 1995 Act applies to Great Britain, Northern Ireland and certain British overseas dependencies. In brief it states that: Any British ship/yacht is *entitled* to fly an undefaced red ensign. British registered ships/yachts (either under Part 1 of the Merchant Shipping Act, or on the Small Ships Register) are *required* to fly an undefaced red ensign (see page 20). Vessels are classed as a 'small ship' if they are under 24m (79ft) long. Equally correct are alternative ensigns whose owners have the relevant Admiralty warrants to fly them (see Ensigns page 19), and an assortment of government ensigns (see Appendix 1).

In the case of British territories, ships registered in a particular territory may fly the appropriate defaced or modified ensign. The same Act states when the lawful ensign shall be hoisted by a British ship 'other than a fishing vessel'.

Flags and the law

When does a British ship/yacht hoist her lawful ensign?

■ On entering or leaving any foreign port.

■ For ships of 50 or more gross tons: on entering or leaving any British port.

■ On a signal being made by one of Her Majesty's ships, including any ship under the command of a commissioned naval officer. (See page 67 for signals.)

Individual nations also have their own specific laws regarding their flags and yachtsmen are advised to make themselves aware of them before arriving in that country. Local bye-laws often exist on rivers and in harbours, and yachtsmen have a duty to establish what they are and to comply with them.

The Law of the Sea

It is impractical to review the laws of every maritime country, however the United Nations Convention on the Law of the Sea (UNCLOS) was adopted in 1982 and signed by 184 countries. It superseded the Geneva Convention of 1958. Vessels belonging to countries which are signatories to the Convention are bound to comply with the Law of the Sea. They also usually have an obligation under their national laws to show their nationality when it is required. Failing to do so can leave the vessel open to being boarded and impounded.

Penalties associated with flag flying

There are penalties for British ships flying the alternative special ensigns without the required warrants, and certain other flags. The other flags which attract penalties include any flags and pennants worn by Her Majesty's ships, and the Union Flag (erroneously known as the Union Jack).

Officials may board the offending vessel, seize the flag and arrange prosecution of the owner or master. The penalty varies but is currently a substantial fine. So a yachtsman who has the cheek to fly a white ensign for instance without holding a warrant for it, would fall foul of this law. Foreign registered yachts using the Union Flag as a courtesy flag in the UK would be incorrect but they would probably be exempt from prosecution under this Act because they are not British ships. Deliberately failing to fly a national flag when it is required, outside or within the UK, can incur a fine of up to £50,000. The officials who may enforce this law are: a commissioned naval or military officer, a Border Agency officer, or a British consul.

It is also an offence for a foreign registered vessel to impersonate a British vessel by flying a British ensign unless she is attempting to escape capture by an enemy. Why it is thought that a British ensign might save a foreign vessel from attack remains a mystery. These days, in certain parts of the world, it is thought that British and American ensigns might actually have the reverse effect, and invite attack!

Hoisting times

Since flags cannot be seen at night, there is no point in having them aloft after dark. Occasionally on land, and sometimes on a vessel in harbour on certain occasions, a flag may be illuminated. The royal standard on Windsor Castle, for instance, is hoisted and floodlit during the hours of darkness.

Hoisting times for ensigns

■ In British water, in harbour or at anchor, the British ensign is hoisted (or made) at 0800 local summer time.

■ In European waters the hoisting time is 0900 between 1 November and 14 February.

■ In American and tropical waters the seasons are less defined and the hoisting time is 0800 all year.

■ In far northern and southern winters, when sunrise is after 0900, the ensign is hoisted at sunrise or follows local custom.

Naval ships and ships with 'ceremonial crews' (for example, training ships) may hoist all necessary flags simultaneously. Yachts and working boats should hoist the ensign first and then work through the other signals, if any. In the case of yachts with British and Commonwealth special ensigns (see page 23), the yacht club burgee must be hoisted before the ensign. In theory, the actual time of hoisting and lowering is taken from any warship present, the yacht club on shore, or the senior (yacht club) officer present.

Lowering (or *striking*) ensigns and other flags is traditionally at sunset around the world. However in high latitudes in the summer, where it may be light almost all night, an arbitrary time can be chosen, usually 2100 local time. If all members of a yacht's crew go ashore before sunset the ensign should be lowered before they leave so that it will not be left flying after sunset, which is not good form. Shore stations and yacht clubs follow the same procedures with ensigns – as if they were a ship moored near that position.

Racing

Ensigns are struck (lowered) at the five minute gun. When the race is over, or the yacht has retired, she raises it again to indicate that she is no longer bound by racing rules.

Timings for burgees and other flags

Customs vary about the timings for flying yacht club burgees, house flags and courtesy flags. The general practice today is for these to be left flying for as long as they are required. So the burgee simply stays up until the owner departs, or for other valid reasons. Some yacht clubs may have rules which require the burgee to follow the same timings as the ensign.

Sometimes the rules state that 'colours shall be hoisted'. (*Colours* is a naval term meaning any flag which displays nationality, usually the ensign or jack.) The best advice is:

- Leave the burgee aloft.
- Lower the ensign for the night.
- The courtesy flag can stay hoisted, which might save problems with a policeman strolling down the dock!

These rules apply in harbour, alongside, on a mooring, anchored in a bay or anywhere else; or even temporarily hauled out ashore.

Lowering at sea

Once out at sea the ensign should be struck. There is no one else to see it and it suffers heavy wear with the apparent wind on the vessel. Under way at night a fluttering ensign is likely to obscure the stern light and make it appear to flash, so it should definitely be brought in. So too should the ensign staff which will cause a blind spot on the arc of the light.

British yachtsmen are not legally required to fly an ensign at sea unless they are signalled to do so by one of Her Majesty's ships (see Law), or by a ship under the command of a commissioned naval officer. This signal is likely to be Code VF ('You should hoist your identity signal') or CS ('What is the name or identity signal of your vessel or station?') If the navy wants you to declare your identity by hoisting your ensign then it is not a bad idea to go along with the request before they use you for target practice!

The burgee stays aloft; but the courtesy flag, if any, is lowered.

Approaching a foreign harbour

During the hours when ensigns are hoisted, all vessels should re-hoist their ensign on approach to a foreign harbour in order to show their nationality as required under international law. Courtesy or Q flags should also be flown if required. See sections on Courtesy and Q flags. At sea it makes sense to hoist the national colours (the ensign) if passing close to another vessel.

In the US, New York Yacht Club rules state that if a yacht enters or leaves port outside the times for hoisting and lowering, but there is enough daylight to sight the flags, then the yacht should show her ensign. It should be lowered once the yacht has moored or reached open sea. This rule seems a common sense recommendation for others, even if not strictly in accordance with all written rulings.

In the days of sailing warships, each position from which a flag was flown had distinct significance, apart from the image of the flag itself. The positions from which flags are flown today are handed down from that time, with modifications. These may vary between sea and harbour.

Commercial ships still have some form of mast, though these have diminished since the days of sail. Even so, it will usually have facilities to hoist the ensign on an aft-facing spar of some sort and signal flags either side. The merchant or other ensign is the most important 'permanent' flag. In harbour (anchorages, rivers etc) on all types of vessel, it is flown from an ensign staff at the stern (Fig 59a). This staff slants aft and is on the centre line unless there is gear that makes this impossible, in which case it should be mounted on the starboard quarter. So at sea on most types of vessel the ensign will be flown on the aft staff or from a spar on the main mast, such as from the end of the gaff boom. Once in harbour the ensign should be moved to the aft staff.

Other ensign positions

Back in the days of sailing ships, the ensign at sea was flown from the gaff of the mizzen. It is still correct on a gaff-rigged yacht to hoist the ensign at the end of the gaff of the aftermost mast (Fig 59a). It does mean, though, that you will have a halyard wrapped across the sail which will require adjustment with the sail (Fig 59c). When the sail is lowered, the ensign will have to be transferred to the aft staff. Another permissible position for a two-masted vessel (ketch, yawl or schooner) is at the head of the aft most mast (Fig 59d).

Modern sailing yachts sometimes hoist the ensign on the backstay because this is near the position of the conventional ensign staff (Fig 60a). This applies especially to racing yachts which try to save weight. It is reasonable, but not very elegant.

Positions of ensigns

Fig 59a Position of ensign on staff at the stern.

Fig 59b Position of ensign on gaff rig.

Fig 59c Position of ensign on leech of sail.

Fig 59d Position of ensign on two-masted vessel.

Fig 60a Position of ensign on backstay.

Fig 60b Position of ensign on yard or gaff.

Ensigns on powerboats

- On powerboats the ensign can be on the same stern ensign staff at all times.
- At sea it can be flown on a yard or gaff specially rigged on the mast for this purpose (Fig 60b).
- Once the motorboat or yacht has entered harbour, the ensign must be transferred to the aft staff. However it does look smart on a yard and this is particularly common on official small craft such as Customs' and harbour masters' launches.
- It may be that a separate ensign will be required for each position because the ensign on the yard is usually smaller than the ensign on the aft staff owing to lack of space.

Seniority of positions

For all vessels it is assumed that there is at least one mast and that this has crosstrees or spreaders). The ensign is never hoisted on the single mast except on a yard. The masthead is reserved for the house flag (for commercial shipping) or the yacht club burgee. It is never used for signals. Thereafter the *seniority* of positions is:

1 Starboard spreader, hoisted close up.
2 Port spreader hoisted close up.
3 Below top flag on the starboard spreader or on starboard inner halyard.
4 Below top flag on port spreader, or on port inner halyard.

Other places where flags may be flown

- On a second mast, ie foremasts or mizzens
- On a jackstaff in the bows

Seniority of ensigns

If you have to place flags below each other on the same halyard, use spans for clarity and try not to offend 'important' flags (see Fig 61).

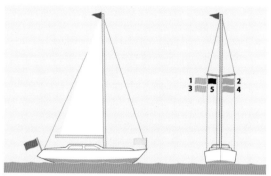

Fig 61 Positions and seniority of other flags.

What goes where?

Problems arise when more than one signal is desired. If there are only two or three completely different flags, then it is quite simple. A sailing yacht may have: an ensign at the stern; a burgee at the masthead (or main masthead); a courtesy ensign at the starboard spreader, if applicable, or another signal, such as a flag of the International Code. However, the situation may not be that easy. Today masthead electronics and other equipment make it difficult to find room for the club burgee so it has to be moved to the starboard spreader, unless you choose options illustrated in Figs 33 and 34.

If a courtesy ensign is needed, it would be discourteous to the country you are visiting to fly it below your club burgee. In this case, the courtesy ensign must be close up to the starboard spreader and the burgee transferred to port. If there is a signal (for instance the Q flag requesting Customs clearance) it can go below the burgee to port (Fig 62).

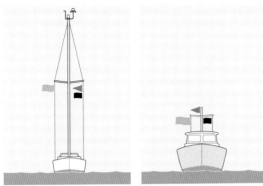

Fig 62 Position of flags on starboard and port spreader (left) and position of flags on motor cruiser mast (right).

The ideal arrangement is to have the burgee at the masthead, the courtesy flag at the starboard spreader and the international signal flag close up to port. Flying the burgee at the masthead does create space when further flags are needed. Techniques for coping with this are looked at on pages 43/4. The same system is used on a motor cruiser provided that she has a suitably rigged mast (Fig 62). If she does not have this, then the flags should be displayed as near as possible to match this pattern.

Certain yacht clubs do not allow their burgee to be hoisted at the spreader or crosstrees: these include the Royal Yacht Squadron and Royal Cruising Club, whose rules insist that you use the masthead.

Positions of other flags

A **house flag** (see page 52) or private signal should be at the starboard spreader (or port spreader if a burgee is already there). In vessels with two masts (sail or power), it should be flown from the head of the shorter mast (not the main mast). It should not be flown at sea, and is usually flown only when the owner is on board. On a motorboat it should go on the stubmast if one is available; failing that it will have to go on the jackstaff.

Burgee on a mastless vessel

If there is no mast: the burgee can be flown from the jackstaff in the bows (Fig 63).

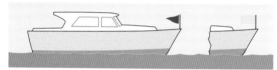

Fig 63 Flags on staff in bows of craft with no mast.

All other flags

Other flags, such as the US guest flags and meal flag, are located in decreasing seniority of positions, starting with starboard spreader, outer halyard as above.

The jackstaff is primarily for what it says, the *jack*. It may, however, carry the burgee on a mastless vessel, and possibly the owner's house flag or 'private signal'. Certain countries have a national jack hoisted there under strict regulations at certain times. Commercial vessels usually have a jackstaff, as do many motor yachts if they have a socket welded on the pulpit. Sailing vessels seldom have a permanent arrangement owing to the requirements of the rig.

Maritime flags ashore

Land flags are not permitted at sea except under particular circumstances, but maritime flags are allowed on shore as long as the establishment is reasonably near the water and that they are hoisted correctly. The exceptions to the 'near water' rule are:

- ◼ Naval establishments well inland
- ◼ Nautical establishments inland (schools for ships' officers, headquarters of pilotage or Customs)
- ◼ Recognised yacht clubs in city locations

SHORE MASTS

These consist of a main mast; possibly with a top-mast; a cross yard or cross-trees; or a yard or gaff. The yacht club burgee or permitted official signal flies from the top of the vertical mast. Halyards run down from the crosstrees for any required signals (including 'reverse' cour-tesy ensign for visiting foreign nationals). The appropriate ensign (naval, national, merchant, yacht, or special ensign) flies from the yardarm and not from the masthead (Fig 64).

Fig 64 Flags on shore mast.

Salutes

As is widely known, but not much practised, flags are used at sea for salutes. It is an international usage and it is the ensign that is used for this; never the burgee or other flags. It is not obligatory but a traditional courtesy. The procedure is to *dip the ensign* as follows:

- ▪ The saluting vessel lowers the ensign about two-thirds of the way down the ensign staff (3).
- ▪ It stays there (*at the dip*) while the vessel being saluted does the same (4).
- ▪ After a pause, she then re-hoists hers fully (5).
- ▪ As soon as this is observed the saluting vessel (6) also re-hoists her ensign (Fig 65).

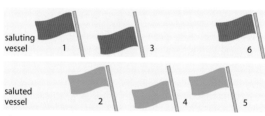

saluting vessel   1   3   6

saluted vessel   2   4   5

Fig 65 Saluting.

Whom do you salute?

- ▪ Salute royal yachts, warships of all nationalities and possibly flagships of great shipping lines (though response is doubtful);
- ▪ Flag officers of your own yacht club, but only on first meeting.
- ▪ Some shoreside yacht clubs (with shore masts) may be saluted once as yachts sail past. 'Once' varies with the club: it might be at the beginning of the season, at the beginning of a regatta, or some other occasion.

- Warships never dip their ensigns to anyone in salute, only in acknowledgement.
- Royal and presidential yachts with royalty or heads of state on board do not return salutes. A yacht saluting a royal or presidential yacht should dip her ensign for 30 to 60 seconds before returning it to the close-up position to ensure that the salute has been seen.

Vessels which take salutes, take them whether under way, at anchor or moored. The ensign must only be dipped by lowering the halyard as described; not, for instance by holding the staff and waving it up and down! A yacht club vessel, on race committee duties, neither dips nor acknowledges any salutes.

Mourning

There is public and private mourning with flags. These consist of hoisting the ensign only at half-mast. There is one exception: see death of the yacht's owner page 91. Strictly speaking the ensign is hoisted to the mast or staff head and then lowered so that it is about one third (not actually half) of the way down the halyard. Note that this is a different position from a *dip salute*. Again, the correct form at sunset is to hoist the ensign fully, pause for a few seconds and then lower completely.

There are also restrictions on *half-masting* the US ensign. Do not half-mast the burgee unless the owner has died.

All vessels in port (half-masting does not apply at sea) should follow local practice. The matter may be for a local or national dignitary. In some countries there are half-mast days for observing a historical event.

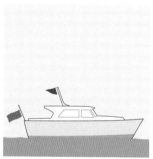

Fig 66 Mourning.

When do you half-mast?

On news of the death, for a number of days afterwards and on the day of the funeral. Yacht or ship owners may wish to mark the passing of someone known personally to them and again the ensign is half-masted (Fig 66).

On Memorial Day, USA (last Monday in May), ensigns are half-masted from 0800 to 1220. A twenty one gun salute starts at 1200 hours and lasts twenty minutes, hence the finish at 1220.

Death of the owner

On the death of an owner of the yacht the ensign, burgee, house flag and stem jack (if used) should all be half-masted from the time of death until sunset on the day of the funeral. The New York Yacht Club, contrary to remarks above, half-masts the burgee (and private signal), but *not* the ensign on the death of a member of the club. Other clubs and nations may have variations. If a salute (dip) has to be made, then the ensign is first hoisted to full height before proceeding.

National mourning

The ensign should be half-masted both when at home and abroad. The stem jack should also be half-masted but the burgee remains aloft.

Hoisting and lowering flags during mourning

If the flags were not previously raised they should be first raised to the close-up position and then dropped down to half-mast position. At sunset they should again first be fully raised for a few moments before being lowered for the night.

Mourning a club member

A deceased club member should be mourned with the club burgee at half-mast on the day of the funeral and on any member yachts of the same club.

Dressing ship

This is a 'flag fiesta' when most code flags are hung out to dry. Sometimes yachts dress overall for a club regatta day – take your lead from the club and flag officers. Vessels often dress overall at their launching or commissioning or when there is to be a ceremony. If, while on a vessel in a foreign port, you find there is an official festival, join in by dressing your yacht.

The recommended order from forward for code flags is: E, Q, p3, G, p8, Z, p4, W, p6, P, p1, I, answering pennant, T, Y, B, X, 1st substitute, H, 3rd substitute, D, F, 2nd substitute, U, A, O, M, R, p2, J, p0, N, p9, K, p7, V, p5, L, C, S. It is suggested that the line up to the masthead ends at '3rd substitute' and starts again towards aft at 'D'.

In the US the order is different and, starting from forward, is as follows: AB2, UJ1, KE3, GH6, IV5, FL4, DM7, PO Third substitute/Repeater, RN First Repeater, ST Zero, CX9, WQ8, ZY Second Repeater.

Dates for dressing ship

In the UK the official dates of celebration and for dressing ship are:

- Accession Day, 6 February
- Commonwealth Day, the second Monday in March
- HM The Queen's real birthday, 21 April
- Coronation Day, 2 June
- HM The Queen's Official birthday: (the date is published annually by signal from the Yeoman of the Admiralty)

In the US two days for dressing overall are: Independence Day, 4 July, and President's Day, the third Monday in February. In France it is Bastille Day, 14 July, and in other countries it is likely to be on days of national celebration.

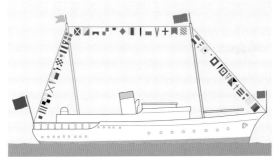

Fig 67 Dressed overall.

How to dress

Flags are flown from the stemhead of the vessel, to a masthead, to any other masthead(s), then down to the after end of the vessel. On gaff rigs, which have not got single backstays, a topsail halyard or a topping lift is used to run flags to the end of the boom and one or two further flags are suspended from the boom and bowsprit ends. The flags used are those of the International Code of Signals plus any other code (eg naval numerals). Certain other flags may be seen in specific positions, as mentioned below, but in the general sequence *no* ensigns, *no* private signals, *no* burgees, *no* inflated fish, streamers or skull and crossbones!

The code sequence for the flags, with the insertion of pennants after every two code flags ensures that a word signal is not inadvertently spelt out. See above for the order of the flags and that the colours are pleasantly contrasting. For etiquette sticklers, there are specific places for ensigns and burgees.

Dressing ship

Masthead ensigns for dressing ships, UK waters

In home waters on a national occasion the yacht's national ensign should be at each masthead and on the taffrail. If privileged ensigns are at the masthead(s) then one must also be on the taffrail. Alternatively you can fly a plain ensign at the masthead(s) and keep your special ensign on the taffrail, but do not reverse this arrangement. The reality of flying national ensigns from your masthead burgee cane will probably be impracticable on the average cruising yacht however, and obviously you can't fly a burgee at the same time. If the person on board is a club flag officer then the flag officer's burgee is flown and not a masthead ensign.

Masthead ensigns abroad

Abroad a visiting yacht which finds herself amidst a national festival should fly the foreign ensign (courtesy flag) at the masthead, or on the foremast of two-masted yachts, and her own national ensign at the taffrail. Any stem jack should also be flown.

Private occasions in home waters

For private local occasions, launchings, regattas, etc in home waters no ensign is shown at the main masthead. Keep the burgee aloft and the ensign on the taffrail and string up the code flags as per above but do not include burgees, house flags, private signals or pennants in the dressing line whatever the occasion. If there are secondary masts they may take further ensigns as above. In all cases the correct national jack (see page 38) may be hoisted on the jackstaff.

International waters

Elsewhere for festivals, the courtesy ensign is hoisted at the 'non-main' masthead, ie foremast or mizzen masthead. The UK ensign is worn at the other mastheads. If there is one mast, it carries the foreign ensign plus club burgee but again to be correct a flag officer flies his burgee and not the (foreign) ensign. We think that, although what is just stated is correct, it would be more courteous to ignore it. In other words, hoist the foreign ensign to the masthead and the flag officer's burgee at the spreader (if, apparently, it is not to be besmirched by an ensign!).

Shore stations

Maritime shore establishments and yacht clubs, provided they have a mast as described earlier with topmast, crosstrees and yard, shall hoist International Code flags in the same way as a ship or yacht. The run of flags can be from near the ground up via the crosstree, across to the mast and down the other side. No ensign is hoisted to the masthead; it remains hoisted on the yard.

Dressing ship is for harbour or anchorage use only. Once the vessel is under way, the code flags should be lowered. However the ensigns remain at the respective mastheads. Ensigns used for dressing ship are not dipped in salute.

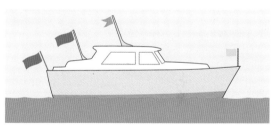

Fig 68 Dressed under way.

Getting it right

Paint it on?

High speed craft such as racing powerboats cannot carry flags in the conventional manner. Painting an ensign or burgee on the hull or super-structure is acceptable but for British vessels it is the ensign which should be painted on and not the Union flag. It is traditional to have a yacht club burgee on a plaque on either bow of a yacht's launch or dinghy.

Burgee rights and wrongs

Yacht club burgees around the world may frequently be unrecognised, but that is no reason for not using them. Generally speaking the view is that a small triangular flag at the masthead or at the starboard spreader should only be a yacht club burgee.

- Don't fly the burgees of more than one club at a time.
- Don't fly burgees or flags that you find in a drawer of the charter yacht if you don't know what they are. They might not be burgees; they might belong to flag officers of a club.

✗ WRONG	✗ NO STATUS	✗ ILLEGAL
unknown regional flag	European Union flag with national colours	Flag of St George

Fig 69 Non-ensigns. Regional and sub-national land flags are not ensigns.

- Do fly your own club burgee on a yacht you have chartered if you want to.
- Do fly your club burgee with its appropriate ensign.
- Do fly club membership flags with another burgee if you like.

Don't

✗ Don't leave large promotional flags flying. They can be very noisy and irritate others who want to spend a quiet afternoon on their boats.

✗ Don't buy cheap printed flags.

✗ Don't fly St George's crosses, Union flags or any other land flags from a yacht.

✗ Don't buy courtesy flags that are offensively small.

✗ Don't offend a senior flag by flying something else above it.

✗ Don't offend a courtesy flag when visiting a foreign country.

✗ Don't fly anything except ensigns or racing flags from the ensign position.

✗ Don't fly ensigns at night under way and obscure stern lights.

✗ Don't fly one country's flag above another.

Do

✔ Lower any flags when you leave the vessel.

✔ Keep them clean and in good repair.

✔ Take them down when not required.

✔ Buy sewn flags and not printed ones.

✔ Make sure you know what is expected when you visit another country.

✔ Make sure your ensign is big enough, but not touching the water.

✔ Ensure courtesy flags are not insultingly small.

✔ Ensure flags are in correct positions of seniority.

✔ Do enjoy flying flags and adding colour to our lives!

Burgees with special ensigns

Pairs of selected yacht club burgees with special ensigns in alphabetical order

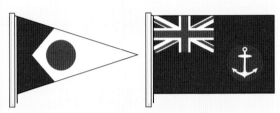

Cruising Association

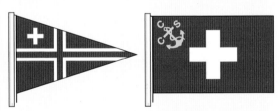

Cruising Club of Switzerland

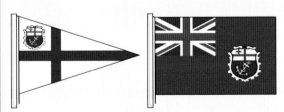

Lloyd's Yacht Club

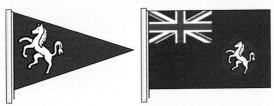

Medway Yacht Club

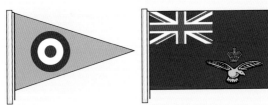

Royal Air Force Yacht Club

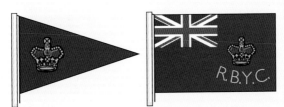

Royal Bermuda Yacht Club

Royal Channel Islands Yacht Club

Burgees with special ensigns

Royal Cornwall Yacht Club

Royal Cruising Club

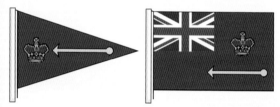

Royal Dart Yacht Club

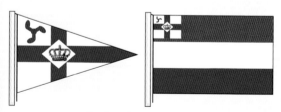

Royal Dutch Motorboat Club

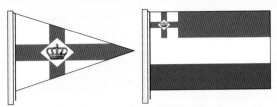

Royal Dutch Rowing and Sailing Club 'De Maas'

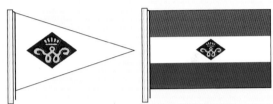

Royal Dutch Sailing and Rowing Club (KNZR)

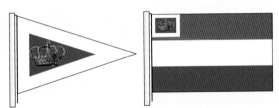

Royal Dutch Watersport Club 'De Kaag'

Royal Fowey Yacht Club

Burgees with special ensigns

Royal Harwich Yacht Club

Royal Lymington Yacht Club

Royal Norfolk and Suffolk Yacht Club

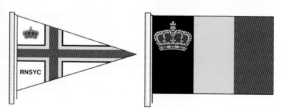

Royal North Sea Yacht Club

Royal Ocean Racing Club Ocean Racing

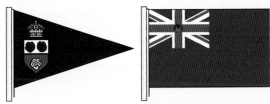

Royal Southampton Yacht Club

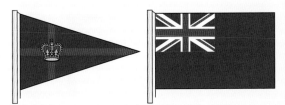

Royal Southern Yacht Club

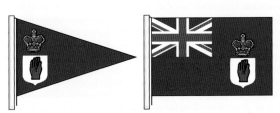

Royal Ulster Yacht Club

Burgees with special ensigns

Royal Welsh Yacht Club

Royal Windermere Yacht Club

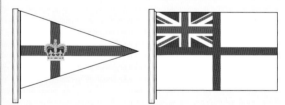

Royal Yacht Squadron

Sussex Yacht Club

Single yacht club burgees in alphabetical order

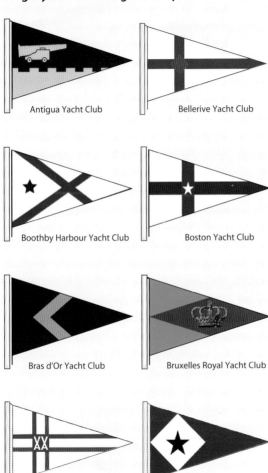

Antigua Yacht Club

Bellerive Yacht Club

Boothby Harbour Yacht Club

Boston Yacht Club

Bras d'Or Yacht Club

Bruxelles Royal Yacht Club

Cercle de la Voile
d'Arcachon

Cercle de la Voile de Paris

International yacht club burgees

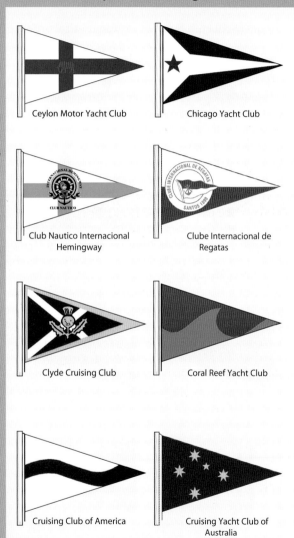

Ceylon Motor Yacht Club

Chicago Yacht Club

Club Nautico Internacional
Hemingway

Clube Internacional de
Regatas

Clyde Cruising Club

Coral Reef Yacht Club

Cruising Club of America

Cruising Yacht Club of
Australia

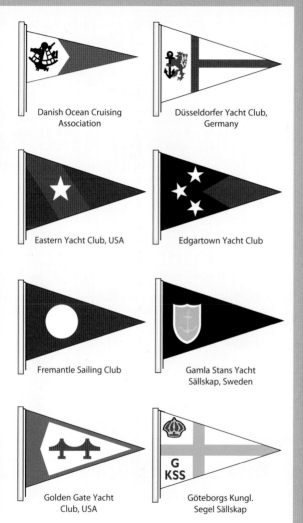

Danish Ocean Cruising
Association

Düsseldorfer Yacht Club,
Germany

Eastern Yacht Club, USA

Edgartown Yacht Club

Fremantle Sailing Club

Gamla Stans Yacht
Sällskap, Sweden

Golden Gate Yacht
Club, USA

Göteborgs Kungl.
Segel Sällskap

International yacht club burgees

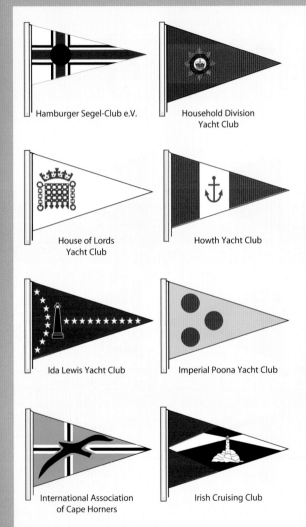

Hamburger Segel-Club e.V.

Household Division
Yacht Club

House of Lords
Yacht Club

Howth Yacht Club

Ida Lewis Yacht Club

Imperial Poona Yacht Club

International Association
of Cape Horners

Irish Cruising Club

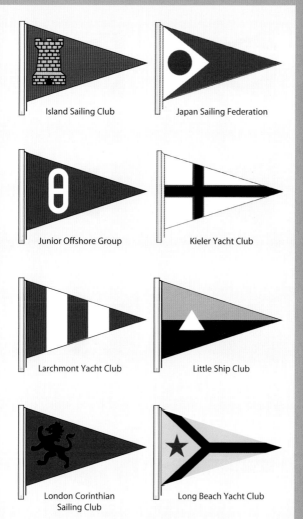

Island Sailing Club

Japan Sailing Federation

Junior Offshore Group

Kieler Yacht Club

Larchmont Yacht Club

Little Ship Club

London Corinthian
Sailing Club

Long Beach Yacht Club

International yacht club burgees

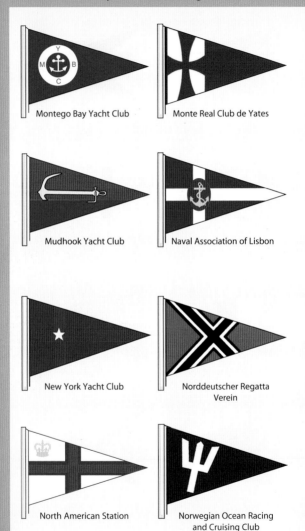

Montego Bay Yacht Club

Monte Real Club de Yates

Mudhook Yacht Club

Naval Association of Lisbon

New York Yacht Club

Norddeutscher Regatta Verein

North American Station

Norwegian Ocean Racing and Cruising Club

Nylandska Jaktlubben r.f.

Ocean Cruising Club

Oxford and Cambridge
Sailing Society

Oxford University
Yacht Club

Point Yacht Club
(South Africa)

Portland Yacht Club
(Maine, USA)

Real Club Maritimo
del Abra y Real Sporting
Club (one of a pair)

Real Club Náutico de
la Coruña

International yacht club burgees

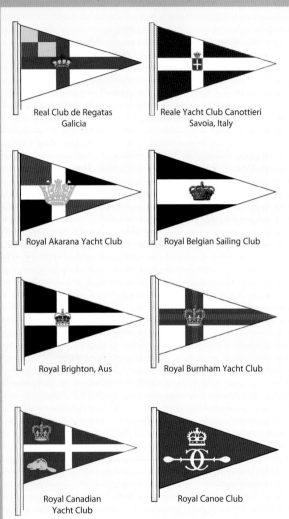

Real Club de Regatas
Galicia

Reale Yacht Club Canottieri
Savoia, Italy

Royal Akarana Yacht Club

Royal Belgian Sailing Club

Royal Brighton, Aus

Royal Burnham Yacht Club

Royal Canadian
Yacht Club

Royal Canoe Club

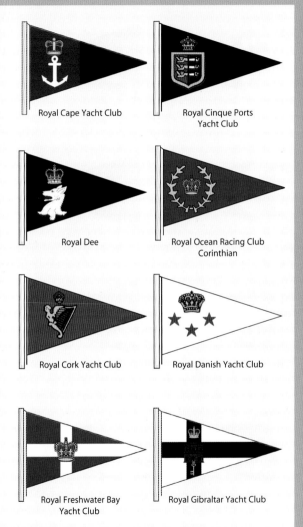

Royal Cape Yacht Club

Royal Cinque Ports
Yacht Club

Royal Dee

Royal Ocean Racing Club
Corinthian

Royal Cork Yacht Club

Royal Danish Yacht Club

Royal Freshwater Bay
Yacht Club

Royal Gibraltar Yacht Club

International yacht club burgeesBurgees

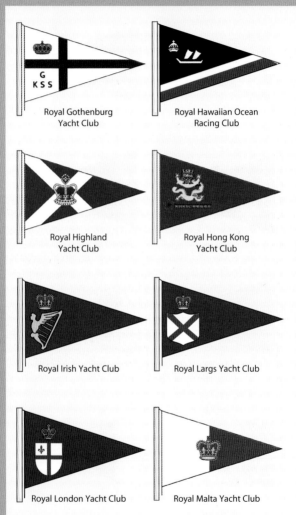

Royal Gothenburg
Yacht Club

Royal Hawaiian Ocean
Racing Club

Royal Highland
Yacht Club

Royal Hong Kong
Yacht Club

Royal Irish Yacht Club

Royal Largs Yacht Club

Royal London Yacht Club

Royal Malta Yacht Club

Burgees

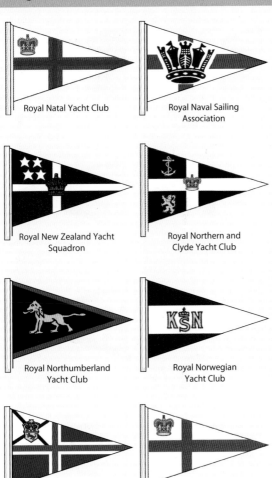

Royal Natal Yacht Club

Royal Naval Sailing Association

Royal New Zealand Yacht Squadron

Royal Northern and Clyde Yacht Club

Royal Northumberland Yacht Club

Royal Norwegian Yacht Club

Royal Nova Scotia Yacht Squadron

Royal Perth Yacht Club

International yacht club burgeesBurgees

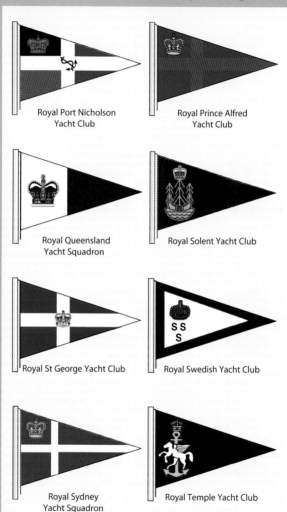

Royal Port Nicholson
Yacht Club

Royal Prince Alfred
Yacht Club

Royal Queensland
Yacht Squadron

Royal Solent Yacht Club

Royal St George Yacht Club

Royal Swedish Yacht Club

Royal Sydney
Yacht Squadron

Royal Temple Yacht Club

Burgees

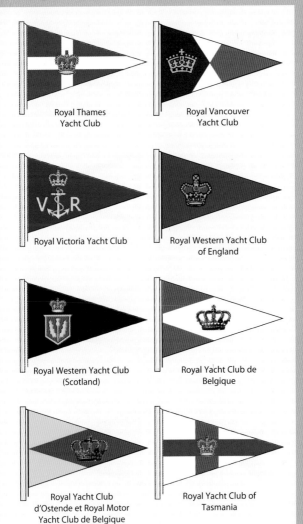

Royal Thames
Yacht Club

Royal Vancouver
Yacht Club

Royal Victoria Yacht Club

Royal Western Yacht Club
of England

Royal Western Yacht Club
(Scotland)

Royal Yacht Club de
Belgique

Royal Yacht Club
d'Ostende et Royal Motor
Yacht Club de Belgique

Royal Yacht Club of
Tasmania

International yacht club burgeesBurgees

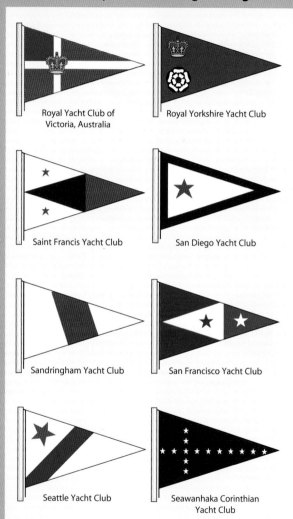

Royal Yacht Club of
Victoria, Australia

Royal Yorkshire Yacht Club

Saint Francis Yacht Club

San Diego Yacht Club

Sandringham Yacht Club

San Francisco Yacht Club

Seattle Yacht Club

Seawanhaka Corinthian
Yacht Club

Burgees

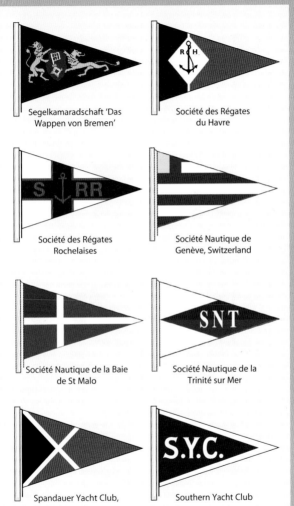

Segelkamaradschaft 'Das Wappen von Bremen'

Société des Régates du Havre

Société des Régates Rochelaises

Société Nautique de Genève, Switzerland

Société Nautique de la Baie de St Malo

Société Nautique de la Trinité sur Mer

Spandauer Yacht Club,

Southern Yacht Club

International yacht club burgees

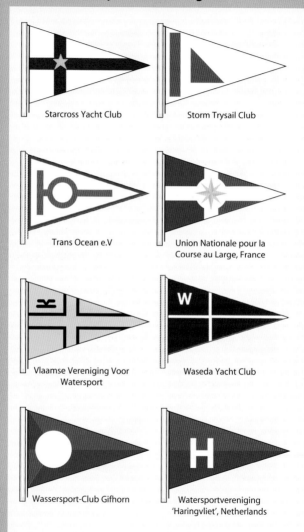

Starcross Yacht Club

Storm Trysail Club

Trans Ocean e.V

Union Nationale pour la
Course au Large, France

Vlaamse Vereniging Voor
Watersport

Waseda Yacht Club

Wassersport-Club Gifhorn

Watersportvereniging
'Haringvliet', Netherlands

Burgees

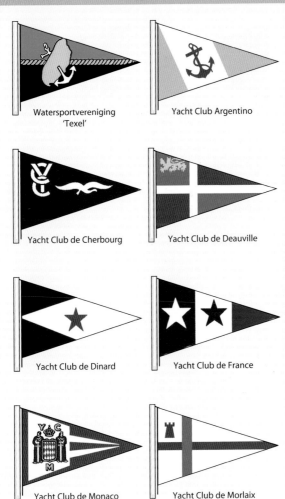

Watersportvereniging 'Texel'

Yacht Club Argentino

Yacht Club de Cherbourg

Yacht Club de Deauville

Yacht Club de Dinard

Yacht Club de France

Yacht Club de Monaco

Yacht Club de Morlaix

International yacht club burgees

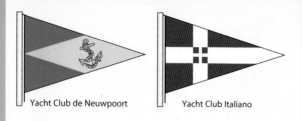

Yacht Club de Neuwpoort

Yacht Club Italiano

Yacht Club Punta Ala, Italy

National maritime flags

Albania

Algeria

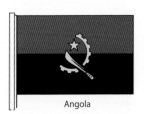

Angola

Antigua and Barbuda

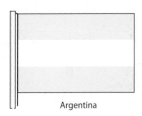

Argentina

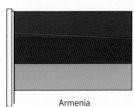

Armenia

Aruba

Australia

National maritime flags

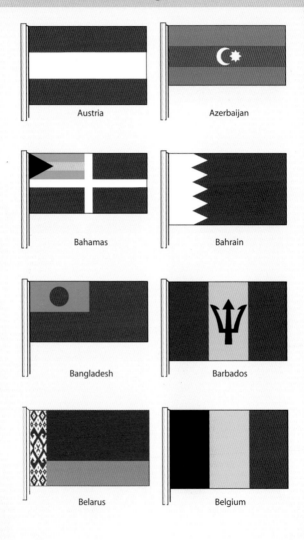

Austria

Azerbaijan

Bahamas

Bahrain

Bangladesh

Barbados

Belarus

Belgium

Belize

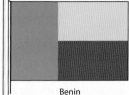

Benin

Bermuda

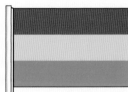

Bolivia,
Plurinational State of

Bonaire

Bosnia and Herzegovina

Brazil

British Virgin Islands

National maritime flags

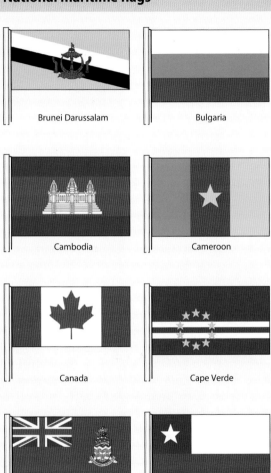

Brunei Darussalam

Bulgaria

Cambodia

Cameroon

Canada

Cape Verde

Cayman Islands

Chile

China

Columbia

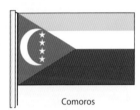

Comoros

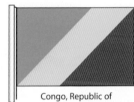

Congo, Republic of

Cook Islands

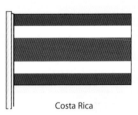

Costa Rica

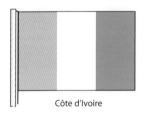

Côte d'Ivoire

Croatia

National maritime flags

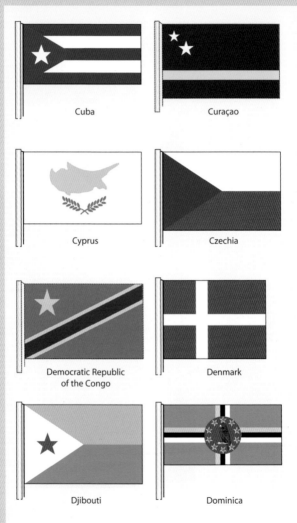

Cuba

Curaçao

Cyprus

Czechia

Democratic Republic
of the Congo

Denmark

Djibouti

Dominica

Dominican Republic

Ecuador

Egypt

El Salvador

Equatorial Guinea

Eritrea

Estonia

Ethiopia

National maritime flags

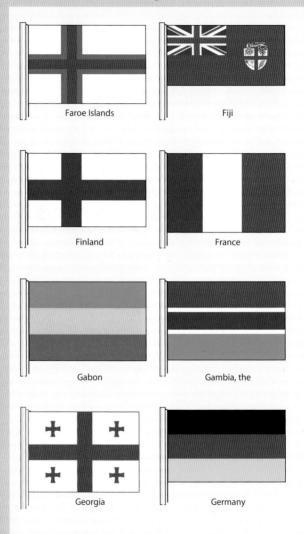

Faroe Islands

Fiji

Finland

France

Gabon

Gambia, the

Georgia

Germany

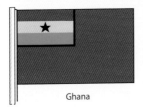

Ghana

Gibraltar

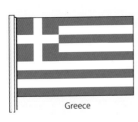

Greece

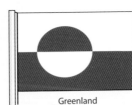

Greenland

Grenada

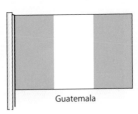

Guatemala

Guernsey
(for use in coastal waters)

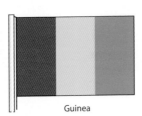

Guinea

National maritime flags

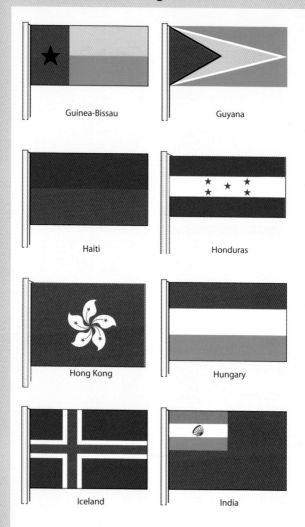

Guinea-Bissau

Guyana

Haiti

Honduras

Hong Kong

Hungary

Iceland

India

National maritime flags

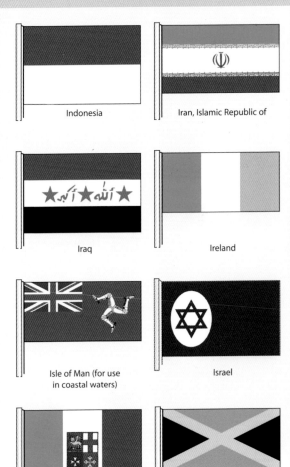

Indonesia

Iran, Islamic Republic of

Iraq

Ireland

Isle of Man (for use
in coastal waters)

Israel

Italy

Jamaica

National maritime flags

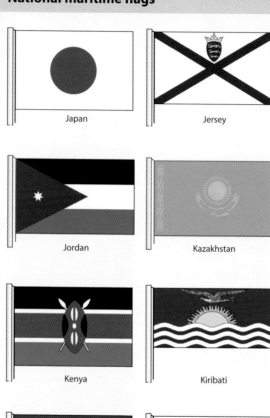

Japan

Jersey

Jordan

Kazakhstan

Kenya

Kiribati

Korea, Democratic People's
Republic of

Korea, Republic of
(South)

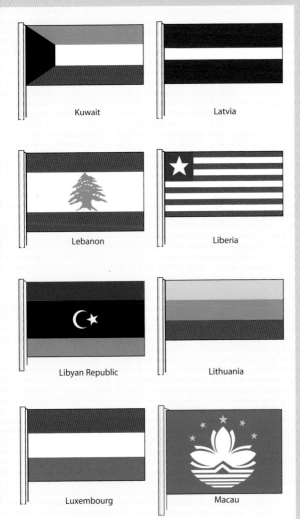

Kuwait

Latvia

Lebanon

Liberia

Libyan Republic

Lithuania

Luxembourg

Macau

National maritime flags

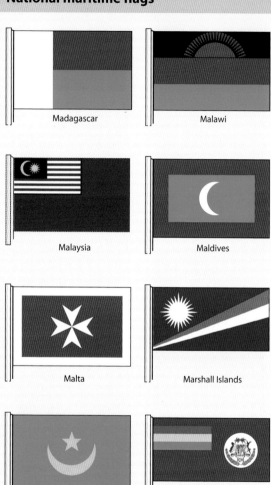

Madagascar

Malawi

Malaysia

Maldives

Malta

Marshall Islands

Mauritania

Mauritius

Mexico

Micronesia

Moldova,
Republic of

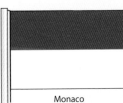

Monaco

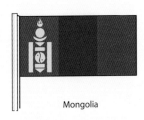

Mongolia

Montenegro

Morocco

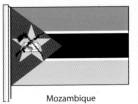

Mozambique

National maritime flags

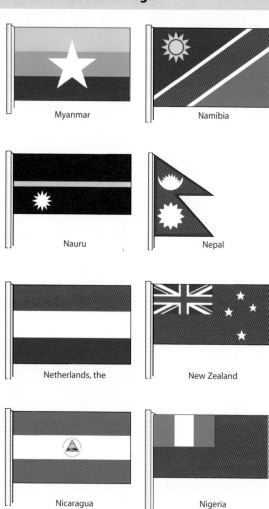

Myanmar

Namibia

Nauru

Nepal

Netherlands, the

New Zealand

Nicaragua

Nigeria

North Macedonia

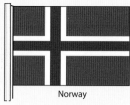

Norway

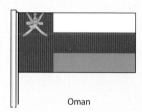

Oman

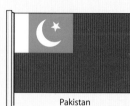

Pakistan

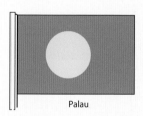

Palau

Panama

Papua New Guinea

Paraguay
(reverse side )

National maritime flags

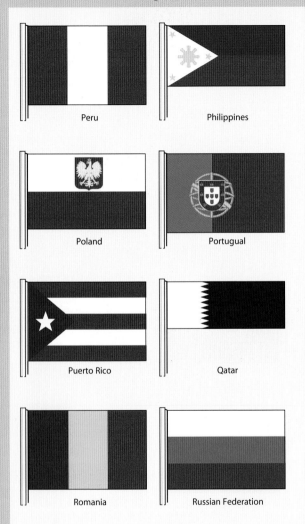

Peru

Philippines

Poland

Portugual

Puerto Rico

Qatar

Romania

Russian Federation

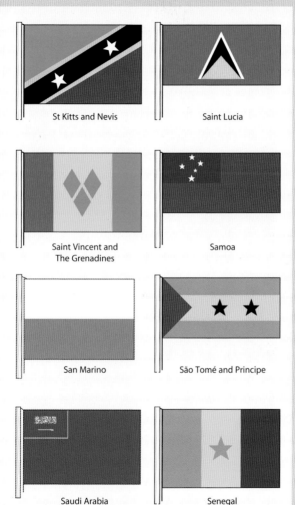

St Kitts and Nevis

Saint Lucia

Saint Vincent and
The Grenadines

Samoa

San Marino

São Tomé and Principe

Saudi Arabia
(reverse view)

Senegal

National maritime flags

Serbia

Seychelles

Sierra Leone

Singapore

Sint Maarten

Slovakia

Slovenia

Solomon Islands

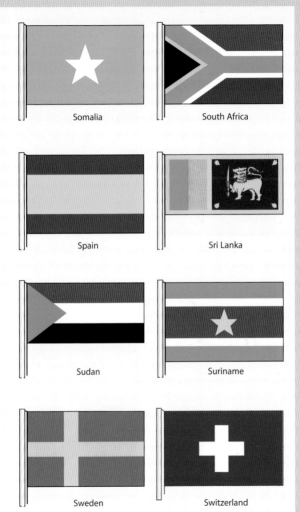

Somalia

South Africa

Spain

Sri Lanka

Sudan

Suriname

Sweden

Switzerland

National maritime flags

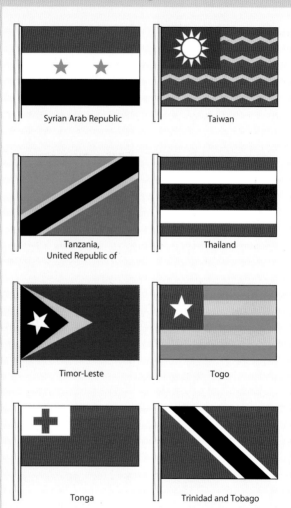

Syrian Arab Republic

Taiwan

Tanzania, United Republic of

Thailand

Timor-Leste

Togo

Tonga

Trinidad and Tobago

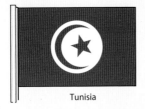

Tunisia

Turkey

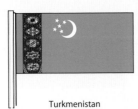

Turkmenistan

Turks and Caicos Islands

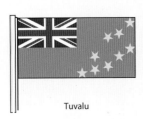

Tuvalu

Uganda

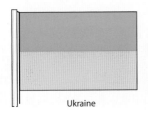

Ukraine

United Arab Emirates

National maritime flags

United Kingdom of Great
Britain and Northern Ireland

United States of America

Uruguay

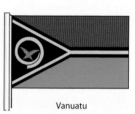

Vanuatu

Venezuela,
Bolivian Republic of

Vietnam

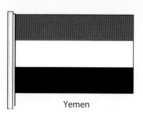

Yemen

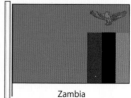

Zambia

National maritime flags

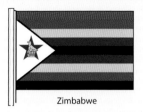

Zimbabwe

International flags

United Nations Organisation*

North Atlantic Treaty
Organisation (NATO)*

European Union*

*Not recognised as a maritime flag but may be flown unofficially with a
national ensign

Glossary of terms

Aft At the back end of a vessel.

Almanac Annual diary containing tidal data and other statistical and astronomical data.

Aloft In the air, up in the rigging.

Answering pennant Used to acknowledge a signal, denote a decimal point, or indicate that the international code flags are in use and not naval signals.

Badge Emblem.

Bermudan rig Single mast with tall, tapering, fore and aft, triangular sails.

Block Pulley.

Bowline Specific knot for marine use.

Breadth The short side of a flag.

Bunting A term for flags and other colourful festive decorations.

Burgee A triangular flag (pennant), usually with a yacht club logo, denoting membership of a specific club.

Canton Upper left hand corner of a flag, ie against top section of the hoist.

Civil ensign A maritime ensign for civilian use, usually undefaced.

Class association burgee A burgee denoting membership of a particular class.

Club association burgee see Burgee

Colours Another term for nautical flags, usually ensigns.

Courtesy ensign A small version of maritime ensign of a foreign country flown by a visiting vessel.

Crosstrees A pair of horizontal poles designed to keep rigging from collapsing inboard.

Defacement, defaced by A badge, device or logo imposed on the design, by way of embellishment.

Device Another term for logo or emblem.

Dimension The long side of a flag also called the 'length'.

Dip salute see Salute

Dress overall, to To decorate a vessel with a full set of the International Code flags along with burgees and ensigns during celebrations.

Ensign A rectangular flag, flown on vessels to represent, and indicate, their nationality.

Evening colours, at Lowering time for ensigns and flags.

Field General background of the flag.

Flag officers A naval term used in yacht clubs denoting rank of certain officials, i.e. commodores, etc.

Fly The outer section of a flag which flaps freely.

Foot The bottom edge of a flag.

Fore and aft sails Modern design sails running from front to back of vessel as opposed to across her.

Fouled anchor An anchor symbol with line entwined around it.

Freeboard Side of a vessel's hull above the waterline.

Gaff Specific pole on head of a squared off mainsail or foresail (but not jib) to maintain sail shape.

Gaff-rigged A vessel having a mainsail (and foresails, but not jib) with a squared off head with a spar to maintain its shape.

Half mast Position on flagstaff or halyard, one third down from top.

Half-masting The ensign, and/or burgee, is raised and then dropped one third in recognition of a death.

Halyard A line for raising and lowering sails or flags.

Head The top edge of a flag.

Hoist The inner, short side of a flag, against the staff or halyard.

Glossary of terms

House flag A personal flag relating to the owner of the vessel.

Inglefield Clip A fastening used for securing flags.
International Code of Signals A set of flags each with an individual meaning, internationally recognised.

Jack A small flag flown only on the bow (mostly naval use).
Jackstaff A rod in the bow of a vessel for the jack.

Ketch Two-masted vessel, the aft mast being smaller than the main mast and located in front of the rudder stock.

Laid up A flag which is no longer in use, but remains on display, is said to be 'laid up'.
Leech The back edge of a sail.

Make, to Alternative wording for hoisting a flag.
Maritime ensign A form of national flag specifically designed for maritime use.
Mast truck Originally a circular wooden cap on the top of a wooden mast with sheaves for flag halyards. A coating of gold leaf indicated that the yacht was free of debt. Modern yachts simply use the term masthead.
Mooring An object secured to the sea or river bed to which in turn a boat may be tethered.
Morning colours, at Hoisting time for ensigns and flags.

Naval code flags An alternative set of code flags used by navies of NATO countries, different from the International Code of Signals flags.

Pennant A triangular flag.
Pilot jack The Union flag with a white border flown on jackstaff.
Port The left-hand side of vessel when looking forward from the stern.

Royal standard A flag or banner with the royal coat of arms, flown by royalty.

Salute, to To dip the ensign two thirds of the way down its staff or halyard and raise again.

Semaphore A message system using hand-held flags.

Seniority of positions The order of rank of importance of hoisted positions.

Schooner Two- or multi-masted vessel with the aftermost mast being taller than, or equal to, the foremast(s).

Sheave A wheel or turning block allowing movement of a line.

Spar Loose term for a yard, boom or mast.

Spreaders More modern version of crosstrees.

Staff Pole or rod from which to fly a flag.

Starboard The right-hand side of vessel when looking forward from the stern.

Strike, to To lower the flag.

Substitutes Three pennant flags (called repeaters in US) denoting repetition of previous flag in a signal.

Swallowtail, swallow-tailed Denoting shape – A rectangular flag with a V section cut out of the fly, which is also sometimes tapered.

Topmast Additional mast above main mast on a gaff-rigged vessel.

Triatic stay A wire that runs from the top of the main mast to the top of another mast; as on ketches, yawls, and schooners.

Undefaced A plain ensign, no logo.

Union canton The Union flag incorporated into left hand upper section (the canton) of a maritime ensign, or other flag.

Union flag, British A rectangular flag representing the Union of Great Britain and Northern Ireland. Shows the crosses of St George, St Andrew and St Patrick.

Glossary of terms

Vexillology A term denoting the study of flags, derived from Latin vexillum.

Yard Wooden pole for maintaining shape of a sail, usually on square sails

Yardarm Outer end of a yard.

Yawl Two-masted vessel, the aft mast being smaller than the main mast and located aft of the rudder stock.

Yacht clubs using a special ensign

White ensign
Royal Yacht Squadron

Blue ensign
Royal Albert Yacht Club
Royal Brighton Yacht Club
Royal Cinque Ports Yacht Club
Royal Cruising Club
Royal Dorset Yacht Club
Royal Engineer Yacht Club
Royal Geelong Yacht Club
Royal Gourock Yacht Club
Royal Highland Yacht Club
Royal Marines Sailing Club
Royal Melbourne Yacht Club
Royal Motor Yacht Club
Royal Naval Sailing Association
Royal Naval Volunteer Reserve
    Yacht Club
Royal New Zealand Yacht
    Squadron
Royal Northern & Clyde Yacht
    Club
Royal Perth Yacht Club of
    Western Australia
Royal Port Nicholson Yacht Club
Royal Queensland Yacht Club
Royal Scottish Motor Yacht Club
Royal Solent Yacht Club
Royal South Australia Yacht
    Squadron
Royal Southern Yacht Club

Sussex Motor Yacht Club
Royal Sydney Yacht Squadron
Royal Temple Yacht Club
Royal Thames Yacht Club
Royal Western Yacht Club of
    England
Royal Western Yacht Club of
    Scotland
Royal Yacht Club of Tasmania
Royal Yacht Club of Victoria

Blue ensign defaced by club badge
Aldeburgh Yacht Club
Army Sailing Association
Bar Yacht Club
City Livery Yacht Club
Cruising Yacht Club of
    Australia
Royal Air Force Yacht Club
Royal Akarana Yacht Club
Royal Anglesey Yacht Club
Royal Armoured Corps Yacht
    Club
Royal Artillery Yacht Club
Royal Australian Navy Sailing
    Association
Royal Bermuda Yacht Club
Royal Bombay Yacht Club
Royal Burnham Yacht Club
Royal Channel Islands Yacht
    Club

Conway Club Cruising
Association
Royal Corinthian Yacht Club
Royal Cornwall Yacht Club
Royal Dee Yacht Club
Royal Forth Yacht Club
Royal Freshwater Bay Yacht
Club of Western Australia
Royal Gibraltar Yacht Club
Royal Harwich Yacht Club
Royal Hong Kong Yacht Club
Household Division Yacht Club
Royal Irish Yacht Club
Royal Jamaica Yacht Club
Little Ship Club
Little Ship Club (Queensland
Squadron)
Royal Lake of the Woods Yacht
Club
Royal London Yacht Club
Medway Cruising Club
Royal Malta Yacht Club
Royal Mersey Yacht Club
Royal Motor Yacht Club of New
South Wales
Royal Nassau Sailing Club
Royal North of Ireland Yacht
Club
Royal Northumberland Yacht
Club
Royal Ocean Racing Club
Parkstone Yacht Club
Royal Plymouth Corinthian
Yacht Club
Poole Yacht Club

Royal Prince Alfred Yacht Club
Royal Prince Edward Yacht
Club
Severn Motor Yacht Club
Royal Southampton Yacht Club
Sussex Yacht Club
Royal Suva Yacht Club
The Cruising Association
The House of Lords Yacht Club
The Medway Yacht Club
The Poole Harbour Yacht Club
Thames Motor Yacht Club
Royal Torbay Yacht Club
Royal Welsh Yacht Club
Royal Yorkshire Yacht Club
Old Worcesters Yacht Club

Red ensign defaced by club badge

Brixham Yacht Club
Royal Dart Yacht Club
Royal Fowey Yacht Club
House of Commons Yacht Club
Lloyd's Yacht Club
Royal Hamilton Amateur
Dinghy Club
Royal Lymington Yacht Club
Royal Norfolk & Suffolk Yacht
Club
Royal St George Yacht Club
St Helier Yacht Club
Royal Victoria Yacht Club
Royal Windermere Yacht Club
Royal Yachting Association
West Mersea Yacht Club

Selected two-code signals

 AC I am abandoning my vessel

 AF I do not intend to abandon my vessel

 AG You should abandon your vessel as soon as possible

 AH You should not abandon your vessel

 AL I have a doctor on board

 AM Have you a doctor on board

 AN I need a doctor

 BR I require a helicopter urgently

 CB I require immediate assistance

 CK Assistance is not/or no longer required by me

 CP1 SAR aircraft is coming to your assistance

 DV I am drifting

 DX I am sinking

 IN I require a diver

IT I am on fire

JG I am aground. I am in a dangerous situation

Appendices

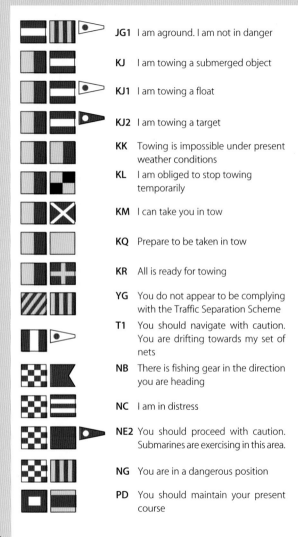

Flags	Code	Meaning
	JG1	I am aground. I am not in danger
	KJ	I am towing a submerged object
	KJ1	I am towing a float
	KJ2	I am towing a target
	KK	Towing is impossible under present weather conditions
	KL	I am obliged to stop towing temporarily
	KM	I can take you in tow
	KQ	Prepare to be taken in tow
	KR	All is ready for towing
	YG	You do not appear to be complying with the Traffic Separation Scheme
	T1	You should navigate with caution. You are drifting towards my set of nets
	NB	There is fishing gear in the direction you are heading
	NC	I am in distress
	NE2	You should proceed with caution. Submarines are exercising in this area.
	NG	You are in a dangerous position
	PD	You should maintain your present course

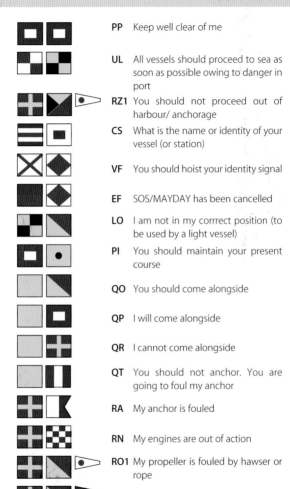

PP Keep well clear of me

UL All vessels should proceed to sea as soon as possible owing to danger in port

RZ1 You should not proceed out of harbour/ anchorage

CS What is the name or identity of your vessel (or station)

VF You should hoist your identity signal

EF SOS/MAYDAY has been cancelled

LO I am not in my corrrect position (to be used by a light vessel)

PI You should maintain your present course

QO You should come alongside

QP I will come alongside

QR I cannot come alongside

QT You should not anchor. You are going to foul my anchor

RA My anchor is fouled

RN My engines are out of action

RO1 My propeller is fouled by hawser or rope

RO2 I have lost my propeller

Appendices

 RY You should proceed at slow speed when passing me (or vessels making signals)

 SQ You should stop or heave to

 UM The harbour or port is closed to traffic

 UN You may enter habour immediately

 UO You may not enter harbour

 UW I wish you a pleasant journey

 VJ Gale is expected from direction indicated (Complements Table III)

VK Storm is expected from direction indicated (Complements Table III)

Useful flag websites

The Flag Institute
www.flaginstitute.org

Flags of the World
www.flagspot.net

International Burgee Registry
www.burgees.com

World Flag Database
www.flags.net

Royal Yachting Association
www.rya.org.uk

Cruising Association
www.theca.org.uk

The World Factbook (CIA)
www.cia.gov/library/publications/the-world-factbook

Information Technology Associates
www.theodora.com

The World of Flags
www.photius.com/flags

Appendices

Overseas territories, departments, crown dependencies, or special administrative regions

American Samoa (USA)

Anguilla (UK)

Aruba (Neth) p. 123

Ascension Island (UK)

Ashmore and Cartier
    Islands (Aus.

Baker Island (USA)

Bassas da India (Fra)

Bermuda (UK) p. 125

Bonaire (Neth) p. 125

Bouvet Island (Nor)

British Antarctic
    Territory (UK)

British Indian Ocean Territory

British Virgin Islands (UK)
    p. 125

Cayman Islands (UK) p. 126

Christmas Island (Aus)

Clipperton Island (Fra)

Cocos (Keeling Islands) (Aus)

Cook Islands (NZ) p. 21, 127

Coral Sea Islands (Aus)

Curaçao (Neth) p. 128

Dronning Maud Land (Nor)

Europa Island (Fra)

Falkland Islands (UK)

Faroe Islands (Den) p. 130

French Guiana

French Polynesia

French Southern and

Antarctic Lands

Gibraltar (UK) p. 131

Glorioso Islands (Fra)

Greenland (Den) p. 131

Guadeloupe (Fra)

Guam (USA)

Guernsey (UK) p. 131

Heard and McDonald Islands
    (Aus)

Hong Kong (China) p. 132

Howland Island (USA)

Isle of Man (UK) p. 133

Jan Mayen (Nor)

Jarvis Island (USA)

Jersey (UK)

Johnston Atoll (USA)

Juan de Nova Island (Fra)

Kingman Reef (USA)

Macau (China) p. 135

Martinique (Fra)

Mayotte (Fra)

Midway Islands (USA)

Montserrat (UK)

Navassa Island (USA)

New Caledonia (Fra)

Niue (NZ)

Norfolk Island (Aus)

Northern Mariana Islands
    (USA)

Palmyra Atoll (USA)

Pitcairn, Henderson, Ducie and Oeno Islands (UK)
Puerto Rico (USA) p. 140
Réunion (Fra)
Saba (Neth)
Saint Barthélemy (Fra)
Saint Helena (UK)
Saint Martin (Fra)
Saint Pierre and Miquelon (Fra)
Sint Eustatius (Neth)
Sint Maarten (Neth)
South Georgia and the South Sandwich Islands (UK)
Sovereign Base Areas of Akrotiri and Dhekelia (UK)
Svalbard (Nor)
Tokelau (NZ)
Tristan da Cunha (UK)
Tromelin Island (Fra)
Turks and Caicos Islands (UK) p. 145
US Virgin Islands (USA)
Wake Island (USA)
Wallis and Futuna (Fra)